TIDES of MISFORTUNE

Maritime Memories from Hull and Grimsby

by

GORDON PEARSON

Foreword
by
Arthur G. Credland

Highgate of Beverley

Highgate Press (Markham) Limited
1995

For Barbara

British Library Cataloguing in Publication Data.
A catalogue record for this book is available from the British Library.

ISBN 1 899498 04 4

Published by

Highgate of Beverley

Highgate Press (Markham) Limited
24 Wylies Road, Beverley, HU17 7AP
Telephone (01482) 866826

Produced by

ba print

4 Newbegin, Lairgate, Beverley, HU17 8EG
Telephone (01482) 886017

Front Cover Picture: The Bayardo *on the Humber sandbank with her back broken (1912)* (Hull City Museums and Art Galleries)

Foreword

This is a remarkable collection of real-life stories of men and vessels associated with the Humber ports of Hull and Grimsby. Neither place has been a stranger to the hardships of making a living from the sea and the author begins in the days of sail when Hull was the home of a great whaling fleet. The *Swan*, missing presumed lost, arrived no less than sixteen months after her departure for the Arctic just as a memorial service had finished on the Dock Green. In the meantime, one at least of the wives of the crew had remarried, not a demonstration of fickleness but as a result of the harsh reality of losing the breadwinner in the days before a welfare system provided financial support.

The author also describes the involvement of two Hull men in the tragedy of the *Titanic*, A. H. Barkworth, a local shipping agent, and Edmond Ryan, both of whom survived, as did another Hull man, J. S. Boxhall, who was Fourth Officer. On a lighter note there is the story of the eccentric *s.s. Bessemer* made to the designs of Sir Henry Bessemer, the steel magnate, for the cross-channel Dover to Calais service. She was far too long and unwieldy to be controllable within the confines of a harbour and, after demolishing a great portion of Calais pier, she was taken out of service and sent to the breakers. This was all without the vessel's primary feature, the 'swinging saloon', ever being tested. This was Bessemer's pet invention intended to prevent sea sickness to which he was a martyr!

The author is to be congratulated on bringing together these records of events familiar and unfamiliar and the many instances of human courage, endurance and determination which they demonstrate.

Arthur G. Credland
Senior Keeper
Town Docks Museum, Hull, 1995.

Contents

Acknowledgements

My sincere thanks are due to the following for much useful information and assistance:

Mr. David Boswell, Mr. David Buckley, Mr. Arthur G. Credland, Mr. Simon Drury, and Mr. Richard J. M. Robinson.

The Staff at Hull Central Library, Grimsby Public Library, Hull City Museums and Art Galleries and Memory Lane, Hull.

The Times (London), *Hull Times*, *Hull Daily Mail, Grimsby Express, Grimsby News, Grimsby Observer, Grimsby Evening Telegraph* and *Fish Trades Gazette.*

The chapter on the *Titanic* is printed with permission of *The Titanic Commutator*, Titanic Historical Society, Indian Orchard, Mass. U.S.A.

Bibliography

Barron, Captain William, *Old Whaling Days* (Hull 1895).

Boswell, David, *Loss List of Grimsby Fishing Vessels* (Grimsby 1969).

Bradley, Leslie, *Four Hull Tragedies* (Hull 1971).

Dorling, Commander Taprell, *Sea Escapes and Adventures* (1929).

Godfrey, Arthur and Lassey, Peter F., *Shipwrecks of the Yorkshire Coast* (Clapham 1974).

Hadfield, R. L., *Sea Toll of our Time* (1935).

Hough, Richard, *The Fleet that had to Die* (1958).

Larn, Richard and Carter, Clive, *Cornish Shipwrecks* (1973).

Larn, Richard and Carter, Clive, *Yorkshire Fishing Fleets* (1973).

Lockhart, J. G., *Perils of the Sea* (London 1928).

Symons, John, *Kingstoniana* (1891).

Wheeler, Harold F. B., *Story of the British Navy* (1931).

Wymer, Norman, *Great Inventors* (Oxford 1958).

THREE HULL WHALING SHIPS

The *Swan*

In the late autumn of 1836, the Hull whaling ship *Swan* was reported missing and long overdue from the Arctic whaling grounds of Davis Straits.

The Hull whalers sailed for the 'fishery', as it was called, in mid-February or March, not returning before September or early October. Unlike the American whaleships which processed or boiled the whale-blubber at sea, the Hull fleet brought home the raw blubber in casks. After several months under hatches the smell from the whaleships' holds as the cargo was unloaded can be imagined.

After mooring in Queen's Dock, Hull, lighters took the casks of blubber up the River Hull to the Greenland Yards near Wilmington, where the whale-oil was extracted. The baleen, or whalebone, was also cleaned there and processed ready to be sent to the manufacturers to be made into a variety of articles, including whalebone stays for ladies' crinolines. Whale oil was a valuable commodity in the 19th century, having been used in the early type of street lighting, before gas superseded the demand for oil lamps. Oil was also needed for a variety of uses in industry.

The reason for the *Swan* not returning to Hull on time was that, in common with a few other daring whaleship captains, Captain Dring had taken the *Swan* further north than usual in a search for whales. The whaling season of 1836 had been a very poor one, with more ice than usual drifting down from the Polar regions. As the *Swan* had taken only three whales during the whole of the summer season, the crew worked the ship amongst the ice-floes of the dreaded Melville Bay in an unsuccessful search for more whales.

It was while anchored to the ice-edge that the crew of the *Swan* saw the whaleship *Margaret* of London

Swan *and* Isabella *by John Ward.*

(Hull City Museums and Art Galleries)

trapped between two huge ice-floes and 'nipped', or crushed, in a matter of minutes.

The *Margaret* was swiftly reduced to a shattered wreck, as the ice-sheet drove clean through the vessel amidships, bringing down her masts on to the ice in a mass of tangled rigging and sails. The *Margaret* sank in 15 minutes, fortunately without any loss of life, but none of her crew had time to save any of their scanty belongings, being lucky to escape with their lives.

It was a rule of all whaleship owners that immediately a ship was lost her crew ceased to be entitled to draw wages. This could be a severe financial hardship on the men's families if the vessel was lost early in the season. Usually, other ships nearby each took on board several of the crew of the wrecked vessel, signing them on as extra crew, and so assuring the seamen of at least a small wage on their return home.

In the case of the whaler *Margaret* of London, six of her crew were received on board the *Swan*, and the men signed articles as crew members. Within six days, the *Swan* herself became 'beset' and frozen into the ice of Melville Bay, with little hope of becoming free before the Spring of 1837. The crew of the *Swan* originally consisted of 48 men, 22 of whom, including the master and officers, sailed from Hull. Two others came from Grimsby, and the remaining 24 were Shetlanders, who signed on at Lerwick. So with the six men from the *Margaret* there were 54 men on board at the time the *Swan* was frozen into the ice for the winter. Little or nothing could be done except make the ship as snug and safe as possible. Attempts were made to saw through the ice-floe and free the ship with twelve-foot ice saws, but as fast as the floe was cleared from the vessel's sides, ice pressure forced the floes to close up, and the gaps were filled again as fast as the men worked.

Rations were reduced, and soon no-one was fit enough to do heavy manual work. Few ships took with them more stores of food than would be sufficient to last until about December of the season in which they sailed. So if a ship was 'beset' in the ice, food had to be reduced, and still further reduced as the weeks passed, to enable the supplies to last as long as possible. In early March, 1837, the ice-floes of Melville Bay began to break free of the main mass, and one such floe, almost half a mile in extent, with the *Swan* still firmly fixed in the centre, began to drift south-west into Davis Straits towards the coast of northern Labrador. It was during this time that an attempt was made to reach the settlement on the coast, but without any success. In fact several of the crew lost their lives in this effort, being cut off from a return to the *Swan*, due to further parts of the ice-floe breaking off and drifting away with the men still on the floe. The loss of the men who attempted to reach the coast affected the rest of the crew who were already in poor health and spirits due to an outbreak of scurvy. Not until late in May, 1837, did the *Swan* finally break free of the ice, and the crew made an effort to set some sails and head towards Shetland. A little while later, in June, the *Swan* was joined by another Hull whaling ship, the *Duncombe*, already home-ward bound from the 1837 season. The master of the *Duncombe* arranged for 20 of his crew to go aboard the *Swan* and help to sail her home to Hull.

In Hull the *Swan* had been given up as lost, as nothing had been heard of her for upwards of a year. On Sunday, 2 July, 1837, a memorial service for her lost crew was held on Dock Green, later the site of Hull's Railway Dock. The service having ended, a collection was taken amongst the gentry for the dependants of the crew, which amounted to just a little over £47. At this very moment news arrived that the *Swan* had been sighted sailing up the Humber! Immediately, the whole congregation rushed down to the river front, and hundreds more assembled at various vantage points to see, and cheer, the long-lost vessel. This was about four in the afternoon, and during the succeeding two hours, while the ship passed through Humber Dock, Junction (Princes) Dock and so into Queen's Dock, hundreds more followed the progress of the ship until she was safely moored in Queen's Dock. The survivors of the *Swan* included her master, Captain Dring and his two sons. The Mate and a few others were in quite good health, but all the men looked rather thin. Of the *Swan*'s original crew of 48, eleven of the Shetlanders had died, seven men from Hull and two from Grimsby. Of the six men from the wrecked ship *Margaret* of London who had gone on board the *Swan* for safety, only one survived the hardships of the voyage.

A local news sheet published the day after the vessel docked, ended with a most interesting piece of news:

'. . . The wife of one of the men belonging to the *Swan*, who anticipated that her beloved husband would not again present himself before her, was, on Sunday last united in the bonds of Holy matrimony to her love stricken swain. On Monday, on hearing of the arrival of the vessel, and the safety of her first husband, she made a precipitate retreat into the country, where, for aught we know, she still remains!'

What the returned husband thought is left to our imagination, for, surprisingly enough, no reporter seems to have interviewed him! As for the £47 collection, history does not record what became of that!

The *Truelove*

Perhaps the best known of the Hull whaling ships was the *Truelove*. She was built at Philadelphia, U.S.A. in 1764, and was captured during the war with our American colonies. She was sold by the British Government in 1780 to a Hull merchant who placed her in the wine trade between Oporto and Hull. Four years later, in 1784, the *Truelove* was re-rigged, greatly strengthened, and converted into a whaling ship. During her long career as a whaler, she made over 80 voyages to Greenland and the Davis Straits whaling grounds without mishap. She was a singularly fortunate ship, being built rather like a barrel, so that when 'nipped' by the ice floes, she would rise up on top of the ice out of danger of being crushed. At one time she lay for six weeks on the ice in Melville Bay, while other less fortunate ships were crushed to matchwood.

In 1849 William Barron made his first voyage on the *Truelove* as an apprentice.

(Hull City Museums and Art Galleries)

Whalers in the Arctic *by John Ward.*

His interesting book, *Old Whaling Days,* published in 1895, gives a valuable insight into the whaling industry of those days. Captain Barron served on the *Truelove* in every position, from apprentice to Master during his career. During the first voyage young Barron made in 1849, the *Truelove* in company with the *Advice*, of Dundee, helped to search for traces of Sir John Franklin's lost Arctic Expedition, missing in the far north since 1845. Lady Franklin had earlier, in 1849, stayed at the Vittoria Hotel in Hull, for the purpose of conferring with the captains of whaling ships bound for Baffin Bay. She hoped that they would agree to land stores and lay depots at her expense, in the various sheltered inlets along that coast.

The *Truelove* and *Advice* put into Lancaster Sound where they landed coals and. dispatches, and erected a marker-post on shore, before continuing their quest for whales. For this attempt to try to aid the missing Franklin Expedition, the Government awarded £1,000 which was shared between the two whaling ships' crews. Young apprentice Barron's share was £1. On his return home, his mother bought six silver teaspoons with the money and had his initials engraved on the handles. Some years ago, these spoons were shown to me by Captain Barron's daughter, the late Miss Lily Barron. The spoons, she told me were still known in the family as the 'Franklin Spoons'.

During the next ten years the Hull whaling industry suffered a decline from which it never recovered. With the scarcity of whales, some vessels frequently took only four or five whales throughout the entire season. A few unfortunate ships returned to port 'clean', not having taken a single whale, and with their crews in debt to the ship. Small wonder that the Hull whaling fleet dwindled year by year, and men and ships began to engage in other more profitable voyages to warmer climates. By the 1860's only the *Truelove* and the *Diana* of Hull remained in the whaling trade, the *Diana* by then having auxiliary steam power.

The *Truelove* left Hull on her final Arctic whale hunt in the Spring of 1868. On her return, she was withdrawn from the whaling industry, and for a few years carried ice packed in sawdust from Norway to Hull and London, for use in the flourishing fishing trade. The east-coast sailing trawlers and drifters having discovered the Dogger Bank grounds, the Box Fleet founded a new trade, and their descendants today sail on modern freezer trawlers to the same Greenland seas their ancestors knew so well.

In 1873 the *Truelove* sailed for Philadelphia, where she was warmly welcomed by the citizens of that port. During her stay, the ship, then 109 years old, was presented with a large silk flag to commemorate her visit. This flag is now in the collection of the Hull Town Docks Museum.

Four years later the *Truelove* was again in the news when six of her crew refused duty, saying the ship was unseaworthy. The vessel, at the time on a voyage from Newcastle to Tarragona, Spain, with coals, put into Torbay, near Brixham. An examiner from the Board of Trade was sent for and he certified the ship was not in a fit condition to proceed on her voyage. In his report he said '. . . on examination of her topsides, I found them sheathed over with wood, and several of the wash-strokes were off. The caulking of her upperworks I found in many places slack. The topsail yards had been sent down on deck; three of them were in a defective condition, the others will require repairs. Also the rigging appears to want a general overhaul. This vessel being loaded with coals and sheathed over with wood sheathing, I a.m. unable a ascertain the condition of her hull and fastenings. During my stay on board she made very little water.'

While the necessary repairs were being carried out, Captain Kidman, the Master, attended court where his six malcontents were on trial. The solicitor for the men offered to pay all the costs if the Master would give the men their discharge, but this Captain Kidman refused to do. The men all appeared truculent, and loudly stated their intention not to proceed with the voyage. One of the men shouted across the courtroom that he would sooner 'do' six months in jail than go to sea in the *Truelove*, as he valued his life more than the money due to him! The Magistrate rose nobly to the occasion, and sentenced all the men to ten weeks imprisonment. After signing on extra men sent from London, the *Truelove* sailed for Spain.

Shortly after this episode, it appears the ship was dismantled and converted into a coal-hulk on the Thames. Nothing more is heard of her until April, 1897, when a schooner ran into, and somewhat damaged, a hulk moored off Gravesend. A report was made to Lloyds, and on looking through their files, in order to record the casualty, it was discovered that the hulk was none other than the 133-year-old *Truelove*. The City of Philadelphia heard of this, and offered to purchase the hulk as a floating museum, with the intention of re-rigging and restoring the ship to her former state. Unfortunately, nothing seems to have come of this scheme: perhaps negotiations were rather slow, before the hulk was disposed of. Lloyds have no further record of the vessel after this, nor the London Chamber of Commerce. The National Maritime Museum had no further information, nor the General Register of Shipping. Here the search ended, and a mystery remains. What was the final fate of the old *Truelove*? Perhaps one day fresh evidence will be forth-coming, but, after this lapse of time, it seems very unlikely.

The *Diana*

In October, 1869, the Hull auxiliary steam whaler *Diana* was wrecked on the north Lincolnshire coast. She was the last of Hull's whaling fleet, which in the early years of the 19th century numbered over 65 ships. The whaling industry in Hull gradually declined after 1820, until in the late 1860s, only the *Truelove* and the *Diana* sailed north after whales. Built at Bremen in 1840, the *Diana* was a vessel of 355 tons. She made her first whaling voyage to Davis Straits in 1856, and thereafter sailed regularly with the other whalers. In 1857 she was fitted with steam power, though still retaining her sail rig. The last three years of the *Diana*'s venturesome career were the most memorable, especially the tragic voyage of

Diana *whaling in the Arctic.*

(Hull City Museums and Art Galleries)

1866-67, when she was frozen up in the ice and compelled to winter in the Arctic. She returned in an appalling condition, almost wrecked aloft, and was called the 'phantom ship'. This voyage of 1866 is worth recalling.

Sailing from Hull, under the command of Captain John Gravill, on 19 February, 1866, bound for the Shetland Islands, the *Diana* reached Lerwick and shipped a number of Islanders as harpooners and extra crew. It was Captain Gravill's intention to try his luck at the seal fishery off the island of Jan Mayen. But, after five weeks, the *Diana* returned to Lerwick; the quest after seals had proved a total failure. She left for the Davis Straits whaling grounds on 8 May, under both sail and steam. At times she made over 10 knots, with all sail and studding sails set. Captain Gravill had never known such a quick passage and on 17 May they rounded Cape Farewell, Greenland. Soon the weather grew worse, and sail had to be reduced, the first ice-was sighted three days later, and the next week saw them off the island of Disco. Whales were seen occasionally, but, although the boats gave chase, they were not successful in taking any until the last day of June, 1866. On that day, two whales were harpooned, towed alongside the ship and flensed. These two whales yielded over 20 tons of oil and 1½ tons of whalebone (baleen), valued at over £2,000. As it turned out, these were the only whales caught by the *Diana* during the season. Fog descended once again. The quantity of ice about compelled the ship to raise steam and break her way out of Pond's Bay, before she became hemmed in with ice. Captain Gravill was reluctant to use the engines as only 30 tons of coal remained in the bunkers.

About this time, the master conferred with those of the other whalers in the vicinity (from Dundee and Peterhead); and it was agreed that the situation was hopeless with so much ice about. Boats could not be lowered to chase the whales, and also the season was far advanced. Accordingly, the ships began to make their way south towards open water. The *Diana* was in company with the Dundee whaler, *Intrepid* (Capt. Deuchars), which was twice as powerful as the *Diana*. The master of the *Intrepid* had promised to stand by the Hull ship until both were clear of the ice. The two vessels were proceeding south, the Dundee ship leading, When a stream of heavy ice-floes came between them, blocking the course of the *Diana*. The *Intrepid* managed to force her way into clear water, and steamed rapidly away to the south, followed by the curses of the *Diana*'s crew. Captain Deuchars said afterwards that he was sure the *Diana* had managed to get clear and was following his lead, though more slowly. Even so, there were hot and bitter words about his action when the *Diana* eventually reached port many months later.

The *Diana* was now alone. Conditions were grim, for the ice stretched away in all directions as far as the eye could see. They had coal left for only two or three days, and provisions which would barely last two months. The ship's carpenter was ordered to cut up the spare topmast as fuel for the engines, and all the unused oil-casks were condemned to be burnt as well, so low had the coal supply fallen. Nothing could be done now that the ice had closed in for the Winter, except drift with the ice pack at the mercy of the winds and currents. By the end of October the *Diana* was off the British colony at Exeter Harbour, Baffin Land. A cresset of blazing tar was hoisted at the foreyard as a signal to the settlers that a ship was fast in the pack, but they drifted past without being seen.

With fuel so scarce the cold penetrated blow decks, and even froze-the medicines in the ship's medicine chests, and every bolt and nail-head in the cabin was covered with thick hoarfrost. Captain Gravill was far from well, owing to lack of proper food and rest. He persisted in remaining fully dressed, and slept on his cabin sofa, ready for instant call should the ship be crushed by the ice pressure against her sides. A quantity of stores and other necessities was kept on deck, ready to be thrown on the ice if the ship should be in danger. All the time the weather remained thick, misty and intensely cold. The ice pressure became so severe that the deck planking was seen to be working up and down, and the ice-floes began 'rafting', one on top of another, as high as the ship's rail. The ice was hourly expected to force its way through the vessel's sides, so boats and stores were hurriedly landed on the ice, and a camp set up some little distance from the ship which was by then almost on her beam ends.

A tent was made from spars and old sails, and the men huddled together for warmth. Although the departure from the ship had been sudden, the master's canary, and a linnet belonging to the engineer were not forgotten, and the two cages hung in the tent near the lamp. A few days later the ice near the tent began to crack, so the crew carried their belongings back on board the *Diana*. She had almost righted herself, and was still seaworthy, though leaking a little. Sawdust was spread on deck, near the pumps, and a sail erected on the windward side to protect the men, for the deck-pumps had to be kept working night and day. This was not because the leak was so severe, but because, if they stopped for many minutes, the pumps froze up completely.

One of-the ship's thermometers had registered 20 degrees below zero for many weeks, but only because-this was the lowest it could register. Captain Gravill had been uneasy for the safety of his ship and his crew. He was unable to sleep, having difficulty in breathing; paralysis of his lower limbs developed, and he sank into a coma. On 26 December, 1866, he died; he was 64 years old.

Scurvy had made its appearance on board in September but there were no further deaths until February, 1867, when the first member of the crew died Most of the coal was now consumed, and almost all the oil-casks. They had even tried burning some of the 'crang' (rotten whale-blubber), in an attempt to keep a fire burning in the cabins, but the fearful black smoke and smell compelled them to abandon this method. The cook was allowed only two coal-bricks and half a cask a day. After the scanty meals had been cooked, he was forced to let his galley fire go out. The canary and linnet still survived though neither of them was very lively. This was not to be wondered, for the cabin beams were thick with solid ice from the condensation of the men's breath. The food allowance had to be cut, and then reduced again. Some of the crew had private stores of food of their own on board, potatoes, tea, coffee and sugar, but all food was collected for the general store at the beginning of the winter, and shared out equally, week by week.

Soon the daily allowance consisted of a half-cooked flour dumpling, fried in rancid whale blubber. The great event of the week was on Sundays, when each man was allocated a whole dumpling, a spoonful of jam and a mug of tea for dinner. Tea consisted of anything they had saved from dinner, plus half a ship's biscuit smeared with the cook's fat, and a mug of coffee. Soup for 49 men was made from five pints of dried peas, with biscuit dust added for thickening.

The casks were all gone by this time, so the main-topmast and the gaff were sent down, and cut up for firing. It was over a year since the *Diana* had left Hull, and, the fuel shortage being so severe, the officers agreed that fires must be kept burning in the cabins at all costs. Anything that could be burned without endangering the ship's sea-worthiness should be used.

At the end of February, still fast in the ice, the ship was off Resolution Island. All tobacco, tea, coffee and sugar supplies were finished, and meals had to be made from the cook's scrap cask, odds and ends of fat and gristle rejected by the men earlier in the voyage, and collected by the cook to be sold as pig-food when they arrived back in port. Most of the Shetlanders were so weak as to be almost unable to leave their bunks. The watch on deck took a very long time to cut up a stun-sail boom for the galley fire, only seven of the crew being unaffected by the scurvy. The men preferred to stay in the cold cabins rather than take exercise on deck to help ward off the scurvy. The surgeon had to order one of the Shetland men on deck where he lay on the ice and moaned to be left to die in peace. When he was allowed to go below, he said to the surgeon he hoped the next time he came up the ladder it would be as a corpse. This poor man survived the winter, but died on the very day the ship reached the Shetlands.

The temperature in the cabins stood at least 22 degrees below freezing, maybe more, and even the lime juice could not be issued. Although the cask had been next to the cabin stove for a week, the lime juice remained frozen solid. In one week the snowfall amounted to nearly seven feet, mounding round the ship until she was almost buried. Five more of the crew had died from scurvy, but in March, 1867, a thaw set in and the ice on the cabin beams began to melt, as did the snow on deck. They were now off Cape Chidley, Labrador. The cabin clock, which had been stopped by the intense cold for many weeks, began to tick away again. The canary and the linnet also showed that they were aware of the change, for they began to sing once more. Both birds survived the voyage, but the linnet was accidentally killed when a crate fell on its cage after the *Diana* reached port. The canary lived on for many years, and, after it had died from old age, it was stuffed and preserved until it was destroyed in an air-raid during the second World War.

All the whale boats except one had been broken up and burned. The davits, sails, oars, spare-topmasts, yards, booms, oil casks and most of the cabin woodwork and cupboards had all gone for fuel, when on 17 March, 1867, the *Diana* at last broke out of the ice-pack and gained the open sea. They were 110 miles off the coast of Labrador, on the parallel of Cape Farewell. After 13 months they were free, and, under tattered topsails, course was set for the Shetland Islands. Three more men died before land was reached on 2 April. Land had been sighted the day before, but, supposing it to be Orkney, the *Diana,* wanting to make Shetland, stood away northwards along the western coast of Shetland, all the time thinking it was Orkney. Next day the Mate decided to put into the first harbour he could find, which happened to be Ronas Voe, and they found they had been off the Shetlands all the time.

The *Diana* remained at Ronas Voe for a week, and during that time three more of the crew died, bringing the total deaths to 13. Provisions and coal were sent on board and, after new hands had been signed on, the *Diana* sailed for Lerwick arriving two days later. All the dead had been buried at Ronas Voe, except for the body of Captain Gravill which was retained on board, and taken with the ship to Hull by the new Master and crew. Some of the sick men remained on board the *Diana* as passengers, whilst the others left for Hull by steamer and train. Still leaking badly, the *Diana* reached Hull on 26 April, 1867, and, as she moored in the old Queen's Dock, flags on the nearby ship were lowered to half-mast and dense crowds looked on, crowding all the vantage points around the dock. The funeral of Captain Gravill took place three days afterwards at the Spring Bank cemetery; his coffin was carried by those of the crew of the *Diana* who were fit enough to attend. More than 15,000 people lined the route taken by the funeral procession.

In the Hull Town Docks Museum there are a number of interesting paintings and relics of the *Diana*, but the most interesting is a flat, dark brown, semi-round object, much worm eaten, one of the few ship's biscuits remaining in the *Diana*'s stores at the end of her tragic voyage.

After being repaired and refitted, the *Diana* sailed once more in February, 1868, for Davis Straits. The voyage was a complete failure, due to the great quantities of drift ice she encountered, and with little wind to disperse it. She returned to Hull on 25 July, 1868, with only three tons of seal oil on board. Great was the surprise at her early return, but rumour had it there was a shortage of provisions, and no-one on board wanted a repeat of the disaster of the previous voyage. At the end of that year, the only other Hull ship in the whaling trade, the *Truelove,* was withdrawn, and used to carry ice from Norway, for use in the local fishing industry.

The following year, 1869, the *Diana* left Hull for the whaling grounds on what proved to be her last voyage. Returning on the 19 October, 1869, she was in tow of a tug at the mouth of the Humber, with a full gale blowing. To safeguard herself, the tug master was compelled to cut the whaler adrift. The *Diana* had the produce of only one whale on board, and, being very light, she was blown ashore near Donna Nook before steam could be raised. All the crew were rescued, but not without difficulty, for some trouble was had before the local lifeboat could be launched, owing to the horses who were dragging the boat to the beach taking fright at the noise of the breakers. The *Diana* was unlucky, she fast settled down, and very soon broke up, becoming a total loss.

Today, somewhere under the sands of the Lincolnshire coast, lie all that remains of the *Diana*, the last of the Hull whaling fleet.

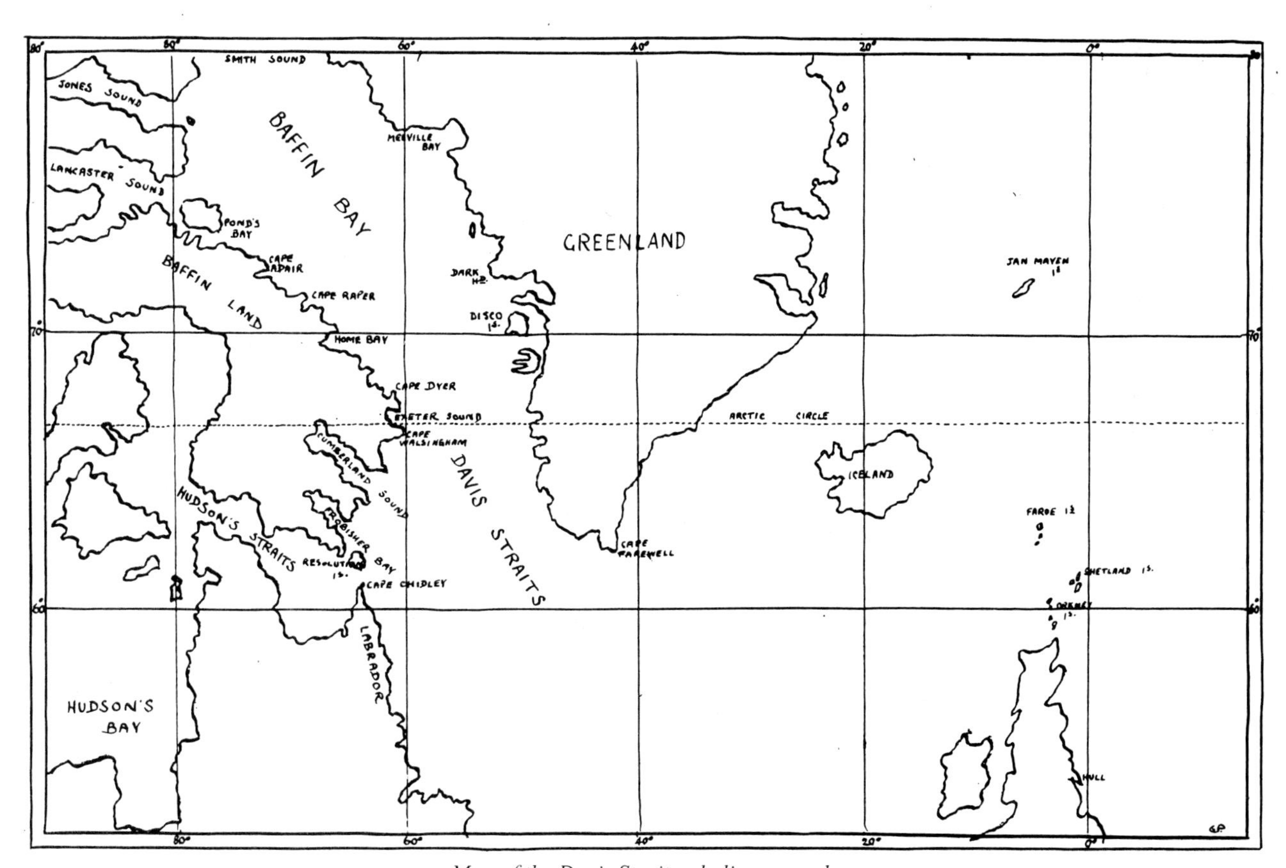

Map of the Davis Straits whaling grounds.

TRAGIC LAUNCHING OF THE *DOWTHORPE*

It was in 1854, while the Crimean War continued, and the Light Brigade charged into immortality in the pages of history and literature, that the *Dowthorpe* was launched from one of Earle's slipways into the calm water of Victoria Dock, Hull. The *Dowthorpe* was an iron barque of some 528 tons, and was built by Earle's Shipbuilding & Engineering Co., Ltd., of Hull, for owners listed as Stuart & Co of Liverpool. She was one of Earle's early vessels, being Yard No. 5. Dimensions were 157.9 x 24.8 feet.

Preparations for the launch had been going on at the yard all the week, and great crowds usually gathered to see the festivities. The time of the launch was to be around 11 a.m. and as early as 7 a.m. people began to make their way towards the yard gates. Well before 11 a.m. there were immense crowds of spectators pressing against the gates and fencing, awaiting admittance. Numbers of them were close relatives of the workers at the yard, and all hoped for good vantage points.

The yard managers had issued special instructions, and precautions were taken to prevent possible accidents. Some of the younger elements in the crowd became impatient and began to climb the fencing, determined to be first inside the yard. As soon as the yard gates were unlocked, the crowd surged forward like a human tide, pushing the heavy gates back, and almost bowling over the two men who were admitting them. The two gatemen had to scramble to one side as the gates swung back into the yard. The crowd broke into a run, and rushed along the rough roadways towards the launch berth. Fences were broken down, and all shouted warnings from the management went unheeded. Several fights broke out between the crowd leaders and some of the yard workers who attempted to restrain the rush.

The decks of the vessels moored nearby in the dock quickly filled with the noisy and excited crowd, and at least 300 spectators rushed up the gangways on to the *Dowthorpe*. They were heedless of the warnings that sitting or standing on the tops of the deck-houses was risky to themselves and the ship, which might become unstable if the centre of gravity was disturbed. Some of the yard workers had to use physical force to clear the decks of the *Dowthorpe* on two occasions. Yet such was the insistence of a number of adventurous individuals that they persisted in returning to their previous vantage points on the top of the deck houses on the *Dowthorpe*.

With her decks and deck-houses crammed with spectators, it is strange that the management allowed the launch to continue. Seemingly it had been a tradition with the other four ships previously launched from Earle's to allow the first arrivals permission to go aboard and be 'launched' with the ship. Such crowds as had appeared for this occasion was unusual. Just after 11 a.m. the ceremony proceeded, and the *Dowthorpe*, duly named by a Miss Baird, glided down the slipways into the water. The ship went straight down the greased ways, but such was the weight of her human cargo, that the vessel took some slowing, and even the bundles of rusty iron chains only just prevented her colliding with the 'dolphin' in the middle of Victoria Dock.

Another tradition was to 'sally' a newly launched vessel, that is to rush from one side of the deck to the other, as soon as the ship was in the water, thereby swaying the ship from side to side. This happened to the *Dowthorpe*. As the cry, 'Let's Sally her!', was heard, watchers on shore saw the vessel begin to lurch slowly from side to side, then more quickly, as the movement of the people continued, One of the two steadying 'check' ropes snapped, and the *Dowthorpe* careered over to starboard. It was at this moment of unusual angle that people who were unprepared for the lurching began to slip and slide across the decks. The more unfortunate ones standing on the unrailed roundtop shot clean off, over the bulwarks and into the water. A number of people standing on the deck on the starboard side were unable to keep their footing as others nearby, caught off balance, cannoned into them, and one or two fell from the deck-house on top of those already slipping. One man and two boys, clinging to the flagstaff at the stern, found it unable to bear their weight, and they all fell into the water when the staff broke off at the base.

Luckily, the one remaining check rope held, and the *Dowthorpe* began to steady herself, but not before at least 100 spectators were left struggling in the water of the dock. The worst danger was to the ones already in the water when others fell from the vessel on top of them. As the accident occurred, there came an awful cry of horror from the quayside and the vessels round about. Confusion and consternation followed as several small rowing boats and timber rafts floating in the dock were steered by volunteers towards the mass of struggling people in the water. The crews of the boats and rafts worked quickly, and rescued spectators were hauled into boats or on rafts. The saved were dumped without ceremony into the bottom of the boats, for there was no time to be wasted in asking questions. A great number were almost unconscious when hauled from the water. Amongst the most active of the boatmen was a lighter man from the *Susan*, named George Barnfather. This man, alone in his boat, rescued no fewer than ten people, pulling them into his boat just as fast as he could. One young boy, thrown from the *Dowthorpe*, landed in the water near an anchored brig. He managed to reach up and grip hold of the rudder pintle with his finger tips. George Barnfather saw him while rescuing others, and called to him to hold on if he could. A few minutes later the boy was hauled to the safety of the rowing boat.

Another rescuer, Richard Murray, who was one of those on the *Dowthorpe*, realised as the vessel reached the water that she seemed unstable with so many aboard. He jumped into the water and swam to the 'dolphin', a distance of about 30 yards, guiding a younger man along with him. After pulling the youth to safety on the 'dolphin', he jumped back into the water again and managed to rescue two others. Hairbreadth escapes were numerous. One man who fell from the poop said afterwards that about 20 others fell on top of him in the water (probably a slight exaggeration!). Only by strong efforts, he said, was he able to shake off the ones who persisted in clinging to him, trying to keep afloat, and so save his own life.

Another man, forced beneath one of the timber rafts, managed by great struggling, to creep out and climb up. He maintained that he left three others still trapped under the raft. The police soon appeared with drags, and boats were plying about for the remainder of the afternoon and into the evening, as no-one really knew how many had been on the *Dowthorpe* in the morning.

On the final accounting it was found that of the great numbers of people who had been thrown, or fallen into the water, only four unfortunately lost their lives.

The names were:

John Simpson (aged 19), ship's carpenter of Davis Square, Bourne Street.

John Jackson (aged 23), riveter, of English Street.

Joseph Lucas (aged 14), son of a hairdresser, lived in Wincolmlee.

John Conlon (aged 24), labourer, of Holderness Court, Witham.

Many of those rescued required medical attention. The boy, Lucas, was already unconscious when he was pulled from the water, but died as he was laid on the dockside on some sacking. The accident to the spectators on the *Dowthorpe* was not the only incident that morning. An old steam-tug, called the *Ann Scarborough*, moored nearby, also had an excessive 'crew' on board her to view the launch of the *Dowthorpe*, and she too was overladen, The tug was well-known as an old and leaky craft, and the numbers on board, rushing into the bows to obtain a better view, soon submerged the bows and foredeck, as far as the paddles, while her stern came clear out of the water. The utmost excitement ensued, but this crowd, realising the danger they were in, rushed aft again, and saved themselves a wetting. They were more fortunate than the *Dowthorpe* spectators, and soon calm prevailed as the tug settled on an even keel once more.

News of the *Dowthorpe* tragedy soon spread into the town. Anxiety made those who knew relatives and friends who had planned to go to the launch gather to gossip and wait on the dockside for the rest of the day, regardless of mealtimes.

The Borough Coroner, Mr. J. J. Thorney, was called, and an inquest opened. After formal identification, the inquest and inquiry was adjourned to give those concerned time to ascertain the condition of the vessel, and the witnesses time to recover from the shock. The inquiry, held a week later, concluded that the *Dowthorpe* would have been more stable had she been ballasted for the launch, and was, without doubt, top heavy due to the excessive number of people allowed to remain on board for the launching. Yet the real cause of the accident, was the simultaneous breaking of the starboard 'check' rope, and the unwise, if traditional, 'sallying', of a vessel whose centre of gravity was unduly high. Had the second 'check' rope not held, undoubtedly the vessel would have completely capsized, and the loss of life would inevitably have been much higher.

At the inquiry, one Thomas Shaw of Lampblack Alley said he took two bodies from the dock about half an hour after the launch, and he had seen several people tumble off the vessel into the water. Police Constable William Darley spoke next, and he said how he was there when the body of John Conlon was found about the middle of the dock. His was the last body to be recovered. Christopher Brown, gateman of the Dock Company, outlined the scene. He was on a steamer on the south side of the dock, very nearly alongside the launch ways down which the *Dowthorpe* came. He noticed the fence being removed from the middle of the ways to let the vessel out. Many people were attempting to climb the outer fence into the yard before the yard gates were opened. He said there was 'a goodly number' of people running across the shipyard area as soon as the main gates were opened, and many ran forward to climb up on to the *Dowthorpe*. A workman with a length of timber in his hands had attempted to stop people climbing on to the vessel, but he was pushed away. At the moment of launching, he heard the crowd on board shouting, 'Get ready to sally her!' As they rushed over to the port side, people began to fall off, while some, he thought, appeared to jump into the water.

Francis Smith, dock gateman (he with the length of timber), said he was at the top of the *Dowthorpe*'s gangway, and estimated there were at least 200 people already aboard. Some were yard mechanics and other tradesmen from Earle's, but most were townspeople. He said he asked people to come off, and waved his piece of timber at them. He was told to mind his own business as they were capable of looking after themselves. Then he was pushed to one side in the scramble for places. Another man from Earle's, at the foot of the gangway, did prevent many from going up, letting just a few pass whom he knew as shipyard workers. In spite of warnings, others climbed up the shore-supports of the cradle, so determined were they to get aboard. He said he warned the ones on the roundtop that there were no rails, and with the least cant of the vessel they would go overboard. It was these people who fell off the roundhouse 'like hailstones', until none were left as the top became too steep to stand on. The final witness, James Wood, who was watching from the deck of a Russian prize vessel, tied up at the dock wall, told how he saw 'at least 60' fall from the top of the deck house when the 'sallying' began. He said it was not a yard rule to ballast new vessels, if, like the *Dowthorpe*, they had not been masted. He confirmed there had never before been such a lawless and determined mob in the yard.

The final verdict:
The obvious cause was found to be the 'sallying' by the crowd on the *Dowthorpe*, and the imprudence of allowing overcrowding on the vessel. The builders were not held to blame in any way, as every precaution had been taken in the yard by the management. These precautions and repeated warnings had been ignored and disregarded by the thoughtless and unruly spectators.

LOST OFF LAMORNA

One of the worst disasters ever to happen along the coast of Cornwall was the wreck of the schooner-rigged two-masted iron steamer *Garonne*, built by C. & W. Earle of Hull in 1866. The vessel was built for William Miles Moss of Liverpool, the owners of a line of steamships, operating from the Mersey ports to the Continent.

The *Garonne* was Yard No. 99, and a relatively small vessel of 638 gross tons, 215 feet x 25 feet and depth 16 feet. She was divided up by four watertight bulkheads, and two partially tight bulkheads rising as far up as the 'tween decks'. Her 90-h.p. engine gave her a maximum speed of roughly twelve knots. She sailed from Bordeaux bound for the Mersey on 21 May, 1868, only some ten weeks after passing a Board of Trade survey. The *Garonne* was valued at a little over £15,000 and carried 600 tons of mixed general cargo. The vessel was under the command of Captain Benjamin Drew, who was a Cornishman from Mevagissy, and had sailed regularly for many years on the Liverpool to Bordeaux run. With the exception of two crew members, one from the Channel Islands, and the other a German seaman, all the crew were English. The ship carried 16 passengers, which included four women, two of them French nurses, and eight young children.

Only a small error in dead reckoning resulted in the loss of the vessel, and this was due to the rotor (propeller) of the log-line which trailed over the stern becoming fouled with strands of kelp. With the log-line becoming unreliable, the Master had to rely on his calculations to plot their position.

At 1.30 in the afternoon of 22 May, Ushant was almost abeam and a third of the voyage to Liverpool was behind them. Captain Drew set a course to take them close by the Longships Light. Towards the end of the afternoon the sun became hidden by clouds, and a misty drizzle of rain began to fall, while visibility deteriorated further as the hours passed. Shortly before nightfall, a seaman who had been sent aft to read the distance recorded by the log-line discovered it fouled with weed and useless. This, of course, meant that the Master was uncertain of the distance run by the *Garonne*, and he had only his own dead-reckoning to plot their position on the chart. Captain Drew altered course once again at 10 p.m. and ordered more sail to be set to take advantage of the favourable winds. The deep-sea lead line had been made ready for use, but, it appeared later at the inquiry, no soundings were taken. By 11 p.m. there still had been no sighting of the Longships Light, and the lookouts were warned to keep alert. Within 25 minutes there came a shout, 'Land – dead ahead!' The wheel was put hard over and the master rang down 'full astern' . Even then it was too late, for, as she turned and heeled over, the *Garonne* struck heavily on the Buck Rocks, barely a mile west of Lamorna Cove. The iron plates tore and crumpled beneath the bridge, and the ship filled and settled in the seas which were breaking over the reef. The Chief Engineer, Alex Ruxton, barely had time to ease the safety valves, when the cold grey sea came flooding up beneath the engine-room plates. He abandoned his post, and he and the other stokers ran for their lives up the ladders to the deck. The first officer lit blue flares and fired rockets, but the distress signals were only seen by the crews of two Cornish schooners, neither of whose skippers realised the lights were from a vessel in trouble.

Captain Drew, Second Officer Wilson, the Bo's'n, the ship's carpenter and other members of the crew began to lower the large port lifeboat and the small cutter. The Bo's'n and the donkey-man climbed into the lifeboat, while the cutter was launched and manned by a fireman and Fred Walker, the cabin boy. The third lifeboat was left in the davits, while the men in the port lifeboat pulled round in the lee of the poop to try and take off some of the passengers. Second Officer Wilson returned to the bridge after seeing the boats cleared away, but saw that Captain Drew and the other officers had left the bridge and were down on the deck amidships. As the *Garonne* was lying extremely low in the water with part of the deck awash, Wilson waded waist deep along the after rails to reach the poop. He was in time to see a large wave wash three of the women passengers over the side, and he dived into the sea to try and rescue them. Wilson was not a very strong swimmer, and luckily for him the cutter appeared close by and pulled him into the boat or he would undoubtedly have drowned.

Confusion continued on board the *Garonne* and attempts were made to launch the ship's dinghy which was slung over the stern, These attempts were hampered by several sacks of green peas, which had been stowed in the dinghy as extra cargo space! The sacks of peas were heaved over the side, and the dinghy cleared and lowered at last. As soon as the dinghy was in the water she began to fill and sink, as there was no plug in the drain-hole. Part of one of the men's shirt was quickly torn up and stuffed into the drain hole as a makeshift plug, and six of the crew scrambled in. It was then discovered that there were no thole-pins for the oars, and so the rope from a floating lifebuoy had to be cut off in length and threaded through the holes and around the oars. All the while, as the dinghy was still taking water, two men had to bail furiously, one with a small bucket and the other with a tin soup plate.

Those of the passengers who had been able to, had reached the poop, and the port lifeboat was pulled under the stern to try and take them off. Unfortunately, heavy seas breaking in high spray frightened the passengers and none would jump into the sea for the men in the boat to pick them up. Less than twenty minutes after she struck, the *Garonne* suddenly shifted on the ledge of rocks, rolled right over, exposing her bilge keel, and then slipped off the Buck Rock into deep water and sank. As there were no signs of any survivors, the port lifeboat was rowed towards the coast, and at dawn the coxwain of the Penzance lifeboat sighted them, and guided the boat into the harbour.

The men from the *Garonne* were escorted to the Ship Hotel, not far from the pierhead, and there they heard the news that the dinghy had managed to reach Mousehole safely. The cutter had not been able to take off the people on the poop of the *Garonne* before she sank, but they had seen Captain Drew on board only minutes before his ship sank. A passing lugger took the cutter in tow off Lamorna and towed her into Mousehole. The wreck of the *Garonne* lay only a few hundred yards from the shore, between Buck Rock and the beach.

The ship must have broken her back as she sank, for by dawn the cargo was already being washed up. Cases and barrels and crates by the dozen were seen scattered along the coast, from Lamorna to St. Loy. Shortly after 9 a.m. the bodies of an eight-year-old girl and her younger sister were discovered in the sea off Lamorna pier. During the afternoon, another lugger from Mousehole recovered the bodies of two small boys, and a fishing boat found the body of one of the French nurses not far from the Penlee buoy. Three other bodies were washed ashore at Lamorna. Two were those of an uncle and his nephew, and the third was that of Captain Drew, his face badly bruised from the rocks. Still more bodies were recovered during the following week, and, as information was being prepared for the inquest, it was very obvious that, while only three of the *Garonne*'s crew had been lost, of the 16 passengers carried, only two survived.

During the subsequent inquiry into the loss of the vessel, Second Officer Wilson, as the only surviving deck officer, was questioned as to why no soundings had been taken as the *Garonne* neared Land's End, and there was doubt as to her actual position. He was also asked about the conduct of the crew who had apparently neglected the passengers, while saving themselves. Wilson had only held his rank for a few months, and, although unsure of himself at the hearing, he denied the accusations that there had been a lack of discipline among the crew. In reply to the query about the soundings, Wilson stated that both the Master and Chief Officer were certain they were only approaching their calculated position, and not over-running it. On his own behalf he maintained that he had jumped overboard simply to go to the aid of the passengers he had seen washed into the sea, and not to save himself. The final word in this tragedy was that Second Officer Wilson was severely censured by the Court, which was rather hard on an inexperienced young man who had the fortune, or misfortune, to be the only surviving deck officer from the ship. No matter what the opinions of the Court, he was not to blame, nor could he alone have been expected to bring order and discipline out of the tragi-comedy of confusion which overshadowed the loss of the *Garonne*.

THE BESSEMER SWINGING SALOON – A SUCCESSFUL FAILURE!

In the year of Brunel's death in 1859, Henry Bessemer established a steelworks in Sheffield where he manufactured steel munitions and rails for the flourishing railway companies. A man of genius and wealth he no doubt gave special attention to Brunel's great 19th-century creation, the *Great Eastern*, a giant vessel of 22,500 tons and almost 700 feet in length, whose size was not equalled until our own time in the 20th century, when the White Star Line launched the *Lusitania* in 1906, which was of 32,000 tons and 790 feet long. The designer of the *Great Eastern* had promised that the sheer bulk of his vessel would preclude any motion at sea in heavy weather and no passenger need fear seasickness. Unfortunately, this forecast was not fulfilled.

Success in steel production, and eventually, in 1873, a knighthood, came to Henry Bessemer, but he had one great weakness – seasickness. This was particularly unfortunate as, on his many business ventures, Bessemer was compelled to travel extensively abroad. Few people suffered more from this illness than Henry Bessemer. On one return voyage from Calais to Dover in 1868, his illness continued after he stepped ashore in England, and during the railway journey to London, and then for more than twelve hours after his arrival home. A doctor was called to Bessemer, and the medical man remained with his patient all that night, but it was many days before he fully recovered. He determined then to do his best to discover some means of preventing sickness at sea, and began plans immediately.

His original idea was really quite simple. It involved a suspended cabin-saloon hung on a system of gimbals, placed at right angles to each other. This he patented in December, 1869. A working model was built on a table, which, by means of a clockwork motor, reproduced the motion of the sea. With the help of this model Bessemer made a number of drawings showing cutaway sections through the saloon which he had already named the 'Bessemer Saloon'.

The drawings were typical of the Victorian age and their creator for they depicted not only the machinery, first in calm water, and then the rolling action, but the 19th-century idea of luxury at sea. Padded leather seats were arranged around the saloon, and around the gallery above. There was a domed glass roof with a circular floor large enough to use as a promenade deck.

The next move was to build a larger replica than the original table-top toy. With the courage of his convictions and the spaciousness of his time, Henry Bessemer drew up plans for a small steamer which would be suitable for carrying his 'Bessemer Saloon'. He entered into a contract with Messrs. Maudsley Sons & Field (Shipbuilders) to build his vessel for £2,975. This contract price had to be increased when slight modifications to the original designs raised the cost of the vessel to £3,061. During the building of the vessel, Bessemer had second thoughts and what he later described as '. . . serious misgivings' about the whole project. It was obvious that his suspended saloon would need

The Bessemer *at Dover (1875).*

(Hull City Museums and Art Galleries)

someone to control it, and there were other modifications which clearly could not be contained in the small vessel he had first designed. He was compelled, therefore, to give up his intention of fitting his suspended saloon in this vessel, and she was sold whilst still on the stocks in an unfinished state. This change of plan cost Bessemer almost £2,000 and his saloon had not even reached the experimental stage. Surprisingly, Bessemer was not discouraged.

One of Bessemer's major difficulties was the fact that, owing to his susceptible stomach, he dare not put to sea himself to supervise his experiments. He had no other alternative but to build a large 'mock-up' in the grassy meadow at the rear of his ornate Victorian house, which he had designed and built for himself at Denmark Hill, in south London, and where he is still remembered by Bessemer Road, named after him. During the early spring and summer of 1869 a succession of engineers visited the meadow behind Denmark Hill. They came to view and test the large contraption about 20 feet square, which represented the midships section of a fair-sized ship, minus bow and stern. The large model was set into the ground so as to allow the grass level to represent the surface of the sea.

The saloon was 12 feet by 14 feet and had seats fitted for about a dozen people. The flat ceiling above formed the 'promenade deck', which was surrounded by a light railing. The whole device weighed several tons, but could be made to roll by a system of rods and shafts which were connected to a steam engine. In this manner Bessemer was able to reproduce the motion of the English Channel without ever leaving dry land, a fact he no doubt congratulated himself upon. But he was not above giving some of his guests a few uncomfortable moments.

When testing his creation, a dozen passengers could suddenly walk together across the deck of the large model and yet make no appreciable difference. For a guiding steersman below was watching a spirit-level, and with a slight pressure on a handle, he could keep his bubble centred and ensure steadiness, while the hull itself rolled as if in a high sea. Should the steersman neglect his handle, even for a moment, then the cabin immediately began to roll as if in Channel gale. This unpleasant motion usually brought forth cries of, 'Stop Her', from the unfortunate passengers who had been enrolled for the tests. After a brief shaking-up, the steersman would restore equilibrium, much to the relief of all concerned.

Henry Bessemer and his associates were of the opinion that this was the invention of a lifetime, and the Bessemer Saloon Company was formed with a working capital of £250,000, an immense amount for those days. Bessemer himself refused to become the Director or Chairman, feeling that this might conflict with his personal interests as patentee, but he did agree to be consulting engineer. To prove he had confidence in his own design, he purchased 10,000 ordinary shares in the company, for which he paid cash. The prior object of the company was to have a steam ferry service between England and France, and the vessels equipped with the patent Bessemer Saloon.

Edward J. Reed, who was later knighted, designed the ship, which was built in Hull by Earle's Shipbuilding & Engineering Company. The vessel incorporated several distinctive features, the most obvious being the extremely low freeboard at bow and stern. The saloon needed at least an area 70 feet by 30 feet amidships, and placed low enough to allow its turning axis to be as near the line of central roll as possible.

Trouble began almost immediately. The engines were to be built by a Greenwich firm, and the representatives from Earle's of Hull said difficulties would arise in towing the ship to the Thames yard for fitting out. Bessemer argued that the ship's engines could easily be sent to Hull in sections, but the builders would not relent, and finally Earle's built both ship and engines. The vessel was Yard No. 197, launched in 1874, and named, of course, almost inevitably, *Bessemer*. She was 349 feet in length and

Interior view of the Bessemer *Swinging Saloon.* *(Hull City Museums and Art Galleries)*

40 feet in breadth, 19 feet in depth and built of iron. Gross tonnage was 1,886.

A further crisis followed, financial this time, and Bessemer had to increase his investment interests to £31,000. The London, Chatham & Dover Railway Co agreed to hire the vessel for short Channel crossing excursions, but the insurance company insisted on a £7,000 premium even before the ship had steamed round from Millwall to Dover. Henry Bessemer had to pay this himself. Due to worry, financial and otherwise, Bessemer's health broke down, and his doctor ordered a complete rest away from drawing board and business. Bessemer was reluctant to trust the installation of his saloon machinery and the fitting-out to strangers, and he would not leave London.

Many people interested in the project expected a utilitarian design for the Bessemer Saloon due to Bessemer's semi-incapacity. But this was an age when the Victorian style of elegance was not only presumed in designs: it was expected to be carried out in practice. The Board, beset with financial cares, would not consider any paring down of their commitments, and they passed with full approval the contracts for fine oak carving, paintings and gilded decorations for the *Bessemer*. The vital question was: would this amazing vessel make seasickness a thing of the past, especially when such vast amounts of money had been lavished on the project?

Trials were to take place on 8 May, 1875, with a full complement of financially interested guests on board. The London, Chatham & Dover Railway Company agreed to allow their Commodore of the Cross Channel Fleet, Captain James J. Pittock, to command the *Bessemer*. Captain Pittock had 20 years of cross Channel experience behind him, and his first task was to have a rehearsal with the ship one fine spring morning in April, 1875. Unfortunately, the famous Swinging Saloon was not ready at this earlier date, so the rehearsal was simply a trial handling of the ship, but the result was disastrous. In a gentle breeze, the *Bessemer* yawed off course and smashed one of her four paddle boxes into Calais harbour pier. The vessel went astern to draw clear, and then steamed at half speed back to Dover. The three weeks prior to the maiden voyage were used in repairing the ship, three vital weeks in which Bessemer had intended to use to perfect the swinging action of his patent saloon.

With scarcely any time to spare, and working both day and night to have the ship repaired ready for the trials on 8 May, it was impossible to perfect the saloon machinery in the time available. Henry Bessemer did not feel he could justifiably subject his guests to Channel crossing in his untested vessel. He, therefore, employed some workmen to rivet plates and girders to the underside of the saloon. This secured the saloon, and made the cabin temporarily non-swinging, and a part of the ship – in fact, a fixed saloon

On the day appointed for the trials the 300 invited guests arrived by special train, and, understandably, disappointed, sailed on the *Bessemer* in a rigid saloon across to Calais. All on board appreciated the seagoing luxury of the vessel, a Cross-Channel steamer said to be far ahead of her time, with carved oak panels, spiral columns, gilded and moulded woodwork, and a painted 'ceiling'. An extremely critical reporter from *The Times*, who sailed with the ship, merely noted that the 1½ hour crossing was better than average, the weather remarkably pleasant, and that the passage had never been made with more comfort to himself and his fellow passengers !

They had not then reached Calais, but many had already decided the vessel was a failure, especially in view of the fact that the much vaunted swinging saloon certainly did not swing. Henry Bessemer must have had mixed feelings on that first crossing, as he had to explain the 'static' saloon, and the quite unexpected calm sea! For which his queasy stomach must have been relieved and grateful.

At 13 knots the *Bessemer* approached Calais harbour, which held the promise of a 'cold collation', the feast so beloved by Victorians when celebrating engineering triumphs. Henry Bessemer, remembering what had happened to his ship the previous time she approached Calais, held his breath while the 'veteran' Captain Pittock issued his orders to the helmsman. Again the *Bessemer* did not respond to the helm, and the vessel smashed at speed into the pier at Calais a second time, breaking off short the huge timbers, and sending sections of the pier rails and decking splashing into the harbour. In five minutes Bessemer was the poorer by £34,000, and he described later it had deprived him of one of the greatest triumphs of his professional life. He had, he said, '. .

fondly hoped to remove forever, from thousands yet unborn, the bitter pangs of the Channel passage'.

No one was injured either ashore or on the *Bessemer*, but the damage done to the pier at Calais was estimated in excess of £3,000. In the subsequent inquiry, the French blamed the incompetency of the seaman in command of the *Bessemer*, and the French were blamed for the inadequacy of the Channel port facilities. The guests from the *Bessemer* took a train for Paris, where the man from *The Times* took the opportunity to attend a race meeting at Longchamps. Next day they all returned. They found the *Bessemer* had suffered only superficial damage, the saloon still in a static state, and hopes waning for a successful trial return voyage.

The bored *Times* man wrote his second dispatch, saying he had enjoyed an extremely good lunch on board the *Bessemer* which was waiting for them on their return from Paris. But . . . as before, the Swinging Saloon did not swing, and they returned no wiser than they went The trial of the *Bessemer* was a failure, but, he thought, an extremely pleasant one.

That report was virtually the end for the ship, and the Bessemer Saloon Ship Company went into liquidation soon afterwards.

Captain Pittock was exonerated from all blame at the close of the inquiry, and Henry Bessemer exonerated himself in his autobiography, which was not published until after his death in 1898. His final word on the subject was that his hydraulic controlling apparatus was never completed, was never tested at sea, and, consequently, never failed.

(Hull City Museums and Art Galleries)

Bessemer *arriving at Calais (1875).*

THE *BURTON* SALVAGE CASE

On Trafalgar Day, 1886, William Smethurst, Master of the Grimsby fishing smack *Burton*, left his home port on what proved to be a most unusual fishing voyage. After an uneventful passage to the fishing grounds, with a following wind, the smacksmen began to put their lines out. The Skipper appears to have been as wily a fisherman as ever pulled a cod out of the sea, and from what later transpired one can only assume he had a determination to bring back to port an unmanned derelict, and so win a salvage award. On Monday, 25 October, when they were about 100 miles east of Spurn, a small brigantine was sighted a little less than two miles away to the S.E. A distress signal was flying, so the *Burton* buoyed her lines and bore away on another tack to close with the strange vessel.

The crew of the brigantine hailed the approaching smack, but were unable to make themselves understood. The brigantine was well down by the head, moving only slowly, with heavy seas breaking over the bows and foredeck. With great difficulty, the Mate and two hands managed to get the smack's boat launched, and they pulled across to the apparently sinking ship. She proved to be a German vessel, the *Burgomeister Oon*. When the fishermen boarded, the Master of the German ship, Henrich F. Hintz, told them in broken English that his vessel had sprung a leak on 24 October, and, while the crew pumped, he had tried to make for the Humber. It was then they saw the Grimsby smack, and sailed towards her, flying signals of distress.

The German captain asked the smack's Mate if he could have two or three of her crew to help with the pumping, as there appeared to be seven feet of water in the forward hold, and about five feet aft. The Mate said he did not think his skipper would agree to this as the vessel seemed on the point of sinking, though he himself had instructions to remain on the *Burgomeister Oon*. Captain Hintz said it was imperative that he obtained some manual assistance, for without help his ship would surely sink. The Mate merely remarked that his skipper expected them to abandon ship, or they would be left to make the Humber alone, as the smack was going to return to the fishing grounds.

The Mate again offered to take off the captain and crew, but the German refused. As the smacksmen were about to return to their fishing vessel, the Mate asked once more if the German and his crew would leave or not. Finally, and reluctantly, as no assistance seemed to be forthcoming, Captain Hintz gave his crew the order to abandon the *Burgomeister Oon*.

The discussion had taken one and a half hours, before the captain of the sailing vessel climbed down into the smack's boat. The Mate remained on the German vessel, and, when the departing captain asked why he was staying, the crafty Mate simply remarked that the boat would come back, for him later! The smack's boat did in fact return to the German brigantine but only to put the second and third hands back on board the *Burgomeister Oon*. A towline was passed across to the derelict and made fast, and, in spite of a strong gale blowing, the smack and her tow succeeded in reaching Grimsby. With the assistance of a tug, and some boatmen, the brigantine was eventually tied up to the dockside. The smack *Burton* then left Grimsby again, and reached the fishing grounds by the following Monday. In the subsequent salvage claim inquiry, held before the Grimsby Admiralty Court, much conflicting and contradictory evidence was offered. The smack's owner claimed £300 as salvage, and William Smethurst, skipper of the *Burton*, stated that without his help the *Burgomeister Oon* would undoubtedly have been lost.

Captain Hintz denied that he had been given any help at all, apart from the tow back to Grimsby, and he also stated he and his crew had left their vessel under compulsion from the Mate of the smack, who had told them that, if they did not abandon ship, the *Burton* would leave them to their own devices. Friedrich Leopold Kracht, the Mate of the brigantine, in his evidence, said that his captain had asked several times to be allowed to return to his own vessel while she was under tow. The skipper of the smack had told him he was 'all right where he was!'

The skipper of the *Burton* said his owners were claiming £300 in salvage fees, and this he thought has very reasonable. Captain Hintz replied that this was far in excess of his vessel's value as she was quite old.

The Court was told that the brigantine was worth only £150, while her whole cargo of 203 barrels of coal tar and 30 tons of pitch was valued at merely £200.

Captain Smethurst of the *Burton* then presented, on behalf of his owners, an itemised account of their salvage claim:

Loss of Fishing time (six days)	£49/19/6	(£49.97)
Loss of 2 tons ice (melted)	£2/00/0	(£2.00)
Damage to smack's boat	£3/00/0	(£3.00)
Food & Provisions provided	£3/00/0	(£3.00)
Towage by Tug	£20/00/0	(£20.00)
Boatmen's fees for docking	£1/02/6	(£1.12)
Further assistance in dock	£2/10/0	(£2.50)
Pumping services, etc.	£18/18/0	(£18.90)
Salvage & crew's services	£200/00/0	(£200.00)
	£300/10/0	(£300.50)

The claim for towing by the tug was put at £20, although the master of the tug *Liverpool* had originally only charged £15! The Court ruled that the value of the assistance rendered by the *Burton* was much less than alleged, and judgement was then adjourned until the next sitting. At the January, 1887, sitting of the Grimsby Admiralty Court held on 21 January before his Honour Judge Stephen LL.D., the case continued with further evidence from Mr. Oates J.P., ship valuer, who gave testimony that in his opinion the *Burgomeister Oon* was valued at only £150 and her cargo at £200. Next to be called was Thomas Sanderson, shipbuilder, and he placed a value of £300 on the brigantine as a seagoing vessel, saying she was very well found, but if compelled to be re-sold by forced sale she would fetch only half that amount.

Robert Mackenzie, speaking on behalf of the smack's owner, showed figures that, by comparison with her earnings on a previous fishing voyage, the *Burton* had lost £50 by her salvage services, and there had been other payments and expenses amounting to more than £68. The value of the smack *Burton* was estimated as being £1,156 and the owners had been threatened with other proceedings to recover the sum of £20, which was then agreed had been made with the Master of the tug *Liverpool* to assist in bringing in the German brigantine.

For the defence the Judge heard Mr. D. H. Bunz, the German vice-consul of Grimsby, who valued the cargo at £125 as it lay in the ship, and the vessel itself at £125. Mr. Hadfield, another shipbuilder, was called for the defence, and he also valued the vessel at £125, adding that it would cost a further £150 to make her fit for sea again. Messrs. Burt, Barton & Heywood, coal-tar distillers of Grimsby, valued the cargo of pitch at £15, and the coal-tar at £75, adding one shilling (5p) for each of the 900 barrels, £45; in all, £135. The solicitors then began to argue and the case was adjourned once again until the February Court.

On 25 February, 1887, the Court sat again to consider the *Burton* salvage claim. However, since the last hearing the brigantine's cargo of pitch and coal-tar had been sold for £150, which left only the value of the *Burgomeister Oon* in dispute. The case was put this time from the human angle that the three men who remained on the brigantine stood to risk their own lives if the vessel had floundered, which at one point seemed likely. The Judge commented that in his view the German crew were perfectly willing to leave their own vessel and go on board the smack, and were under no duress to leave. Regarding the master of the brigantine, he said he did not come to the conclusion that he showed any great desire to re-board his ship. It was known that once he left his command he would undoubtedly lose his certificate, but that was his misfortune!

As to the value of the *Burgomeister Oon*, the German vice-consul wrote some figures on a piece of paper, passed it across and asked if that amount would be of any use. The plaintiff's solicitors replied quickly that it certainly would not as they claimed £200. The items of expenses were questioned for some time before finally the Judge awarded the salvors £100 for expenses and £100 for pure salvage services: this was one third the value of the vessel and her cargo. With that the *Burton* salvage case concluded, perhaps not without some relief from all concerned, but with little consolation for the smack owners who lost face over the trial, and had £100 deducted from their original claim.

NARCISSUS IN DECEMBER

Wednesday, 16 December, 1886, was a great day for the inhabitants of Hull, and especially for the yard workers of Earle's Shipbuilding & Engineering Company Ltd., for this was the day chosen for the launching of *H.M.S. Narcissus*, one of the waterline armour belted cruisers which the Government of the day had decided to order two years previously from the Hull shipyard. The occasion of the launching ceremony had been the talk of the town for some weeks past due to the importance of the event, as the vessel was of a class not previously constructed by the local shipyard. It was also hoped that the completion of the contract would mean further Government orders being awarded to Earle's in the future.

The date of the launch had been fixed for the morning of the sixteenth, as this was the best daylight tide for two months. Unfortunately, the weather for several days previous to the launch date had been really vile, with grey skies and much heavy rain. Daylight on the Wednesday came only to show there was to be no change in conditions, and little chance of a fine day. Rain had fallen continuously almost all the night, and torrential rain fell during the morning, continuing through the ceremony and long after everyone had departed. Hurried consultations among the yard manager's staff resulted in awnings being erected to give a little comfort to the launch party and guests. There was also some attempts made at warming, virtually useless, but done with the old pattern of Victorian copper foot warmers, filled with hot water.

At first light, carriages and a great variety of horse-drawn vehicles began to arrive at the shipyard entrance with invited guests. Hundreds more people arrived on foot and there was much competition for good vantage points which also provided some semblance of shelter from the downpour. Such viewpoints were rare, and the majority had to stand out in the rain, and also in at least an inch of oily mud. However, the Victorian middle class were a hardy breed, and were used to a little mud in their daily work.

The launch was due to take place at exactly 8.30 a.m. but, long before daylight on this cold, dark December morning, men had been busy clearing away timbers and greasing the ways ready for the launch event. The platforms at the bow and sides of

(Royal Naval Museum, Portsmouth)

H.M.S. Narcissus – *launched at Earle's in 1886.*

the *Narcissus* were crowded with important personages and ticket holders, while the viewpoints which offered any shelter at all were crowded with thousands of spectators. *Narcissus* had been decked with flags from stem to stern since the previous day, while St. George's ensigns were flying, or, more properly, hanging wet and bedraggled at both bow and stern and amidships. A rather sorry and saturated Union Jack hung from a temporary staff erected on what was later to be the fore-turret.

As the time drew nearer 8.30 a.m. vantage points were at a premium, and several other vessels under construction were used as platforms by the yard workers who stood out braving the rain without any shelter whatever, apart from sacks and odd pieces of canvas around their shoulders. Below them, the yard was a sea of black cloaks and umbrellas belonging to the crowds, many of them standing in thick mud, or on greasy insecure baulks of timber, waiting for the ceremony to begin. At 8.15 a.m. the Vicar of Drypool, the Rev. J. Beddow, commenced the short introductory service which took place at the launch of all naval vessels. As this was concluded, the managing director of Earle's responded by reading the 107th Psalm. Mr. F. B. Grotrian then spoke a few words, followed by Mrs. Grotrian.

After a few more ceremonial speeches, kept short by mutual consent in deference to the rain which thundered on the awnings and poured off in a constant stream on to the boots of the nearby spectators, all was ready for the launch. The yard manager shook his head to the signals, pointing to his little gang who were having trouble with some of the timbers. With almost all the ship's weight now resting on some vital beams, there was great difficulty in freeing the last dozen or so timbers which had become swollen by the heavy rains of the previous few days. Not until almost 9 a.m. did word come from below the platform that the launch could take place, as all but two vital timbers were released.

The wife of Mr. C. H. Wilson M.P. was to do the honours, and as she left her seat she was presented with a huge ornate pair of scissors with which to cut the ribbons. The scissor handles were in the form of the flower after which the ship was to be named, and were contained in a navy-blue velvet presentation case. After cutting the retaining ribbons, Mrs. Wilson then proceeded to swing and break the bottle of wine against the bows of the cruiser, wishing '. . . success to the *Narcissus*'. As the bottle broke against the bows, the last block was freed on the launching ways, and the warship moved slowly down the ways in the pouring rain, to loud cheers and shouts from the gathered crowds. The Band of the Artillery Volunteer Corps played *Rule Britannia* and then quickly changed, after some slight hesitation, to the National Anthem as the ship finally floated free into the River. Although the storm of rain and low grey skies made the occasion extremely unpleasant, the rain and the north wind had brought a very high tide as predicted, and so all went as planned, although a little behind time due to both ladies, who of course insisted on making their speeches in full regardless of the wishes of their lords and masters.

The company then dispersed, the invited guests driving to the Royal Station Hotel for a warm, and no doubt very welcome, late breakfast, which apparently lasted until the early afternoon!

The contract for the *Narcissus* had been placed with Earle's in April, 1885, the Company having previously been placed on the Admiralty List as suitable for naval contract work. The vessel was one of a number of cruisers being built at the time by various yards throughout the country. Palmer's on the Tyne were fitting out the warships *Orlando* and *Undaunted* in 1888, and Napier's were building the *Australia*.

The *Narcissus* was 327 feet in length (300 feet on the water-line), with a beam of 56 feet and a displacement of 5,000 tons. She was designed for a service speed of 19 knots from engines of 8,500 h.p. driving twin three-bladed screws. Armaments were two ten-inch breech-loading guns on central pivots, bow and stern; ten six-inch breechloaders amidships, five each side, in un-armoured turrets. In addition she had auxilliary armaments of 14 quick-firing Hotchkiss guns in the main 'tween decks. The vessel was not to be fully rigged, but when completed had two pole masts with Gatling guns in the round tops. The bow had the inevitable ram of cast steel so beloved by the Victorian warship designers, which was more ornamental than functional, and was part of the standard design of most warships over the heavy cruiser class.

The armour above and below the waterline was of ten-inch steel manufactured by Messrs. John Brown a Co., of Sheffield. The coverage of this armour extended along the whole length of the engine-room and boiler spaces, including of course the magazine. Extra protection was given by wing bunkers of coal along both port and starboard side of the engine and boiler spaces. A complete steel protective decking extended fore and aft above the armour belt, and the openings in this deck were protected either by armoured hatches and shutters, or armoured steel gratings. An armoured pilot-house forward on the upper deck was fitted with a protected communications system to the bridge and engine-room. Provision for the crew was forward of the officers' quarters and in total was for 420 officers and men.

A number of watertight compartments and steel bulkheads acted as another measure of security for the vessel in the event of her being holed in several places at the same time. Her designers declared proudly she would have a good chance of remaining afloat should such an event take place!

A new feature was in cabin fittings consisting of the substitution of thin steel for cabin bulkheads in place of .panelled and carved woodwork previously thought to be indispensable by Victorian ship designers. A throwback to the Nelson era still remained for the crew, in so much as many of them slept in hammocks in the 'tween decks, with an arrangement of netting in which to stow hammocks, bedding and personal ditty-bags during the day. The idea being, as in Nelson's *Victory*, that the stowed night gear around the bulkheads would act as protection and shelter from rifle bullets. This would, in reality of course, have been of little use in sea warfare in the late 19th century.

One unusual feature of the *Narcissus* was that Earle's also built and supplied the engines and boilers for the vessel. Previously it had been usual for Thames-side firms to supply all machinery for warships built for H.M. Government, whether built by private firms or even in the Royal Dockyards. At the time of the launch of the *Narcissus*, the definition of a belted cruiser was '. . . a vessel of war, capable of great speed and having an armoured belt of protective steel at the waterline'. This type of armed vessel was not intended for coastal defence, but for the protection of merchant ships and for attacking an enemy's commerce and sea-trade.

In 1875 Earle's had built the *Valparaiso*, (later renamed *El Blanco Encalada*), for the Chilian Government, and it was confidently stated in 1886 that, while the *El Blanco* had defeated the *Huascar* in an action off the South American coast, the new *Narcissus* could easily dispose of the *El Blanco Encalada!*

With the successful completion of the *Narcissus* in 1887 Earle's Board of Directors confidently looked forward to being awarded further Government contracts for more warships. These followed in 1891 when Earle's launched the *Endymion*, and again in the following year, 1892, when the *St. George* went down the slipways into the Humber.

COLLISION

One morning in late November, 1887, the Hornsea coastguard was on routine patrol, when through his telescope he saw what appeared to be a fishing smack's boat half a mile off shore and heading towards the breakers. Four men seemed to be in the boat, three of them bending over the oars to prevent the boat from broaching. The alarm was given, and the lifeboat was turned out, but some time was taken in collecting and harnessing the sixteen horses required to pull the heavy boat in its wheeled cradle down to the beach.

In a remarkably short time the pierhead was crowded with spectators, many of whom ran down to the beach either to see, or help launch, the lifeboat. In fact the lifeboat was never launched on that occasion, for the cradle's wheels sank deep into the soft sand and shingle, and the bows of the boat became embedded in the sand. While in that position, three waves struck the lifeboat in quick succession, and she broached, turning broadside to the beach.

The smack's boat was, however, exceedingly well handled. The watching crowds saw her turn head to sea, and then quickly rowed stern first towards the beach. The first man to jump out, waist deep in the water, proved later to be the Skipper. He then grasped the stern, while the Mate prepared to follow him, but he was thrown into the water by the lurching of the boat which caught him off balance. Two further crew men came to the stern, leaped out, and one was grasped by the coastguard who had organised a human chain, some standing waist deep in the waves, to pull the men from the breakers, The second-hand had his feet dragged from under him by the undertow, and stumbled on his hands and knees in the water. Fortunately, he was quickly dragged out by the rescuers, as a particularly high wave came up the beach, lifted the now empty ship's boat, and dropped it on the beach, on to the very spot where the second-hand had been kneeling only seconds earlier.

The rescued, but now very wet crew, were taken to the Marine Hotel in Hornsea for some hot food, rest, and a change of clothing. The vessel whose crew had been saved so dramatically was the Grimsby trawling smack *Bellerophon*, 54 tons, owned by Messrs. Long, Little & Jackson; her master was John Wyatt.

The smack had left Grimsby bound for the fishing grounds of the Silver Pits, in a light headwind, then had to beat off the land. The following day, the weather remained clear, but with occasional showers, a choppy sea and a strong wind blowing from the north east. They were about 14 miles from Flamborough Head, and on the port tack heading S.S.E.

The Second Hand, William Pye, was on watch and he saw the lights of a steamer approaching, so he called out Skipper Wyatt. The steamer was almost dead ahead, but unaccountably she altered course to cross the bows of the sailing smack. The ship had three masts and appeared to be a collier, rather clumsily handled, as she seemed to be making as much leeway as headway, and should, in any case, have given way to the sailing vessel. The steamer bore down on the smack, and with a crash tore off her bow-sprit. The crew hailed for assistance after the collision, but received no reply from the steamer. Someone on the smack lit a flare on the Skipper's instructions, while others ran forward to view the damage. They saw that the bowsprit and much of the stem had been torn out, and the water was already rushing into their vessel. She was clearly down by the head only moments after the impact.

The crew were unable to use the steam-pump, as it was first necessary to light the boiler to get steam up, and they had barely managed to coax the wood alight before the rising water put out the fire. The *Bellerophon*'s crew continued to light flares, and shout and hail the steamer, but the distress signals were ignored, and the dark mass of the steamer vanished in the darkness as she continued on her course. The steam-pump was impossible to use, and the hand-pump was not powerful enough to cope with the inrush of water from the damaged bow, so the Skipper ordered the small boat to be launched. The men made an attempt to go below and collect some of their personal gear, but they found the water in the cabin was already up to the tops of their sea-boots. All hope of saving their belongings was given up, and the sinking smack was abandoned by the Skipper and his three men crew.

They left the smack at about 1.30 in the morning, but did not row too far from their sinking craft. A very high sea was running, so three oars were lashed together, tied to the painter and dropped overboard, to act as a sea anchor. This enabled them to keep head to sea until daylight, when the lights of another steamer were seen, and more flares lit, but this steamer apparently did not see the smack's boat, half hidden in the troughs of the waves. The steamer kept her course and disappeared. The *Bellerophon* had sunk by this time. The crew saw that she was still afloat half an hour after they left her, but she was extremely low in the water. Then her masthead light suddenly vanished, and she seemed to go down on an even keel. At full daylight, with a clear horizon, and no other vessel in sight, the skipper decided to cut the sea-anchor adrift and row in towards the land, as the wind and tide seemed favourable. After several hours of hard rowing, they at last managed to reach the shore, where they were assisted on to the beach at Hornsea, but with no idea of the name of the mysterious steamer which had run them down in the night. Later events proved the steamer to be the *Dalbeattie*, 896 tons, registered at Middlesbrough, John Gregory, Master. On arrival at Middlesbrough, one of her crew volunteered a statement that the ship had been in collision with a fishing boat during darkness, and proceedings were instituted against the *Dalbeattie's* Master and owners. The inquiry into the running down of the fishing smack *Bellerophon* by the *Dalbeattie*, was convened in Grimsby on 12

(David Buckley Collection, Fleetwood)

Grimsby trawler China *– built in 1893. An early steam trawler similar to the* Sando *and* Chilian, *the* China *was not scrapped until 1936.*

January, 1888. The steamer had left Liverpool, via the Channel, on 18 November, bound for Middlesbrough in water ballast, with a crew of 18. The *Dalbeattie* was steaming at full speed, but, being in ballast, she was light and rolling heavily. At 11.55 p.m. a fishing vessel under sail was seen about 150 yards off the bow by the look-out on the steamer.

In his evidence, Captain Gregory of the *Dalbeattie* said that the fishing vessel was without lights, but he immediately ordered the man at the wheel to port his helm, while he rang down to stop the engines. As far as he observed, the smack appeared to pass safely astern. The Captain gave his opinion that no collision had taken place, and not even the paint was scratched on his vessel. In direct contradiction of Captain Gregory's evidence, one of the steamer's crew said he was on the foredeck of the *Dalbeattie*, and he definitely heard the crash as they collided with the smack, and it must have been then that the fishing vessel lost her stem and bowsprit.

In judgement, the Court of Inquiry found they were very concerned about the conduct of the master of the *Dalbeattie*, especially the fact that he had not notified, or made a report to, the authorities in Middlesbrough. This, the Court said, was reprehensible, and much more should have been done at the time of the incident. The Official Report said that it was not incumbent for the Court to deal with the Master's certificate, but regarding the duties of the Second Officer, it must be a lesson to him to be more vigilant in the future.

The Master of the fishing smack *Bellerophon* was in no way to blame for the loss of his vessel. The Court concluded their findings by stressing Section 16 of the Merchant Shipping Act of 1873, regarding the conduct of Masters of ships which were in collision at sea.

Although the smack's Skipper was exonerated, the findings of the Court must have seemed small enough compensation to the smack owners, who had suffered the loss of their vessel, in circumstances which were beyond the control of her Skipper.

THE *SANDO*'S ICELANDIC SAGA

The steam cod-fishing vessel *Sando*, owned by the then newly formed White Star Fishing Company, left Grimsby with a crew of twelve men, on 12 November, 1889, bound for the cod fishing grounds off the north coast of Iceland. Twelve days later word arrived in her home port that the weather conditions on the fishing grounds were exceptionally severe for that time of the year, and the *Sando* had last been sighted making for the shelter of a fjord.

No further news was heard of the *Sando* for close on three months, and the owners assumed that the vessel and all her crew must be presumed lost. Then on 11 February, 1890, a packet of letters was received from the Master of the *Sando* and members of her crew. The letters were written from Seydisfjordur on the east coast of Iceland, and dated 15 December, 1889. The Skipper stated in his letter how the *Sando* had sustained a great deal of damage and that a member of the crew had been lost overboard in a storm. The ship's boat and compass had been lost, and, in addition, a part of the bridge and engine-room skylight had been carried away. The owners learned that the damaged *Sando* was still anchored in a sheltered Icelandic fjord, and so arrangements were made to send out the *Sudero*, another vessel belonging to the same company, with stores and facilities for emergency repairs, as soon as she arrived back in port.

Two weeks later, when the *Sudero* docked in Grimsby from a fishing voyage, and her catch had been discharged, these arrangements for the relief of the *Sando* were put into operation. Extra provisions, a spare compass, spars and other necessities were sent aboard the *Sudero*, and she sailed for Iceland on 26 February, 1890. After meeting with her sister-ship, and transferring the stores and supplies, the Skipper of the *Sudero* had instructions to continue on a fishing voyage, while the crew of the *Sando* made their own repairs. It seems that this part of the programme was not carried out for some reason.

There was great excitement in the port of Grimsby when the two steam cod-liners *Sando* and *Sudero* eventually returned home on 26 March, 1890, as the *Sando* had then been absent for almost five months. As such a length of time had passed without news, it had been concluded early in the New Year that the vessel must have been lost in the violent winter storms. Consequently, the wages of the crew had been stopped as was usual when a ship was lost. The wives and dependants had been given grants from the Widow's and Orphan's Relief Fund, and in fact this support was continued in the mistaken belief that the crew had been lost, until the first news of their survival arrived in early February, 1890.

On Saturday afternoon, 26 March, 1890, when both the *Sando* and the *Sudero* were expected hourly, both dock piers were thronged with noisy and excited watchers, many of whom had waited for hours since just after dawn. By the time the returning vessels were sighted, thousands were lining the fish-dock jetties. The two steam cod-liners were seen to be flying numerous pennants and flags. First into the dock was the *Sudero,* closely followed by the *Sando* whose flag was at half-mast as a token of respect for the unfortunate William Brown, who had been lost overboard during the winter. As soon as the two steamers had been safely moored to the jetty, hundreds of the watchers jumped on board, cheering, shouting and waving hats, scarves and handkerchiefs. The crowds swarmed over the decks, shaking hands with the returned crews, and the bells of nearby churches began to ring a welcome.

A detailed story of all that had happened to the *Sando* came from a news reporter who interviewed members of the crew. The *Sando* left Grimsby on Tuesday, 12 November, 1889, and, without encountering any particularly bad weather, the ship reached the Icelandic cod fishing grounds late on the following Saturday night.

A strong gale began shortly afterwards, which compelled the *Sando* to seek shelter in a fjord for six days. When the weather improved, the vessel left the fjord to continue fishing. The *Sando* was line-fishing for cod and managed to get in only two days fishing before a northeast gale blew up with very thick weather of sleet and snow. It was extremely risky and very nearly impossible to steam landward for shelter in a fjord, due to the blizzards and dangerous coastline. So course was altered, and the *Sando* steamed further out to gain sea-room to ride out the storm. On 24 November, 1889, the weather began to worsen, and about half past eleven in the morning course was again altered, this time towards the Faroes. It was then, just as the vessel was turning, and was almost broadside on to the seas in altering course, that they shipped an immense sea. The crew saw the huge wave rise on the quarter, almost as high as the masthead, loom darkly over them, and then fall with tremendous force across the vessel.

William Brown was at the wheel, and he put up one hand as if to ward off the weight of water, but he was carried overboard and lost. Part of the open bridge disappeared, together with the wheel, the main gaff, the mizzen boom, the cabin skylight and the top of the engine-room skylight. A steel ventilator was sheered clean off at deck level, the cabin door stove in, and the clock, barometer and all three compasses were washed overboard. The ship's boat, spare sails, spars, etc., all vanished in the welter of white water, leaving the decks of the *Sando* swept almost clean. The cabin and the engine-room were several feet deep in water and the stokehold fires were extinguished. The crew were all dazed, but surprised to find they still had a deck under their feet.

The pumps were started, but after only half a dozen strokes the pumps seized-up and became useless. This left the cold and numbed crew with the only alternative of baling out the water by hand with buckets, for 23 consecutive hours in relays. The Chief engineer went below and ran off eight gallons of oil, so that, as the water was baled out and thrown overboard, the oil spread around the ship, and had the effect of calming the waves slightly. It also meant, of course, that the crew had to bale out the engine-room in filthy conditions, with oily water slopping on to them as the buckets were passed up the ladder. The following day, the water below decks had been reduced sufficiently to enable the engineer to raise steam again, and course was set for Iceland, which was visible occasionally through the intermittent snowstorms.

The *Sando* dropped anchor in Faskrudsfjord at about six o'clock on the evening of 26 November, 1889. The weather was still severe with showers of driving sleet and snow, and the freezing sleet froze to the decks, rigging and superstructure on contact, and the *Sando* was soon completely covered with a sheet of ice. Standing on the heaving deck was extremely difficult, and the crew found their soaking wet clothes actually froze upon them, and their clothes became so stiff that working and bending became almost impossible. The Skipper sent ashore to the nearest habitation and managed to procure a spare compass but this turned out to be worse than useless, as it had apparently not been used or adjusted for some considerable time.

The vessel then steamed north along the coast to Seydisfjordur which seemed to offer more shelter than the rather exposed fjord they had been moored in. The crew managed to obtain some little assistance from a number of Icelandic fishermen and attempted to make slight repairs to their ship. They also obtained from these Icelanders a pole-compass and attempted to set a course for home. But once again they were unsuccessful, as this second compass had not been adjusted either, and the *Sando* had to return once again to Seydisfjordur. On 15 December, 1889, all the crew except one wrote letters for home, and the Skipper engaged an Icelandic fisherman who was willing to walk to Reykjavik with them. This involved a walk of about 330 miles over wild, rugged country, but it was the only way to get a message through to the capital so as to catch the mail-boat for England.

The crew put together various amounts of money and gave the man the value of 65 Icelandic Kroner to carry the letters: this would be about £3.50 in our present currency. The crew were reluctant to use this method which was uncertain to succeed, and might possibly be unreliable. But there was no other way of getting the packet of letters to Reykjavik, apart from the messenger they had engaged. Many of the rough tracks and ill-made mountain pathways would be blocked by snow, and quite often the man would have to find alternative routes along narrow ledges; paths where no pony would be able to find a foothold.

On 17 December, 1869, a fierce blizzard and terrific gales swept the area, and nine of the wooden houses in the nearby village collapsed under the weight of snow and wind pressure. The *Sando* dragged her anchor and was swept down the harbour before sufficient steam could be raised to get her back to a safe anchorage. The crew were living on the vessel, with occasional forays ashore for water and other necessities, and were apparently very well treated by the 600 or so villagers who lived at Seydisfjordur.

Some food was obtained from the Norwegian Agent at Seydisfjordur and the villagers had a number of ancient muskets, rather like an English blunderbuss, with which they shot a kind of white partridge, possibly a ptarmigan, to help feed the *Sando*'s crew. Time hung heavily on the crew's hands as they waited for a relief vessel to come to their aid. All the men realised that, even if their messenger reached Reykjavik safely, it might be some weeks before help arrived, in response to their letters home. In actual fact, the letters were delivered in Reykjavik, and mailed to England. The rescue vessel sailed from Grimsby; arrived in Iceland, and effected repairs – all this before the lone messenger returned to Seydisfjordur, after his long walk of 660 miles!

About 8 a.m. on a clear morning of hard frost, a ship's steam whistle was heard echoing from the rocky cliffs, and a steamer was sighted entering the fjord. The vessel was the *Sudero*, sister-ship of the long absent *Sando*. The *Sudero* was herself almost a floating iceberg, every rope, spar and rail was covered in ice, which in places was almost 18 inches thick on the foredeck. It took two days of hard work to chip away the ice with axes and crowbars, before stores for repairing the *Sando* could be transferred. When repairs were finished, and the *Sando* was seaworthy once more, the two cod-liners raised steam and set course for home. On two occasions severe weather compelled the two steamers to put back, and, on the second forced return, they found their messenger had returned from Reykjavik, and he reported he had delivered the packet of letters to the mail-boat! He also said he had a very rough journey both ways.

About 15 March, 1890, the homeward voyage was recommenced, and both vessels managed to put in four days' long-line cod fishing off the Faroes, although only nine score of halibut were caught. During their enforced stay in Iceland, they hardly ever saw the sun the whole time, and had only five hours of daylight in 24. When the weather did clear at night, the Northern Lights were often very brilliant, and this enabled hand fishing to be carried out by the crew, which helped conserve food supplies. After their return to Grimsby on 26 March, 1890, an official dinner was arranged in honour of the crew of the *Sando*. Their families and friends were also invited to celebrate their return home after an absence of almost five months. The Mayor of Grimsby, Alderman H. Bennett J.P., presided, together with a large gathering of town councillors and members of the local clergy.

Some little time later, a local artist, G. V. Burwood, was commissioned to paint a seascape showing the *Sando* being struck by the tremendous heavy seas. The painting apparently portrayed the steam cod-liner *Sando* in the trough of the waves, her boat and pieces of timber spars etc., being swept overboard. The painting was on exhibition in the shop window of Jenkins & Remy's, carvers and gilders, Victoria Street West, Grimsby, for some weeks. One wonders if the painting still exists somewhere, in private ownership, or a local art gallery.

Sando: Sunk in collision with s.t. *Oceanic* of Grimsby, 19 July, 1911, about 25 miles S.E. of Munken Light, Faroe Islands.

Sudero: Stranded and lost, 30 April, 1903, Sarclet Head, Caithness.

WHEN SAMUEL PLIMSOLL CAME TO GRIMSBY

This notice was printed in the Grimsby News for 22 March, 1890.

> SAMUEL PLIMSOLL
>
> Wants to see some of the Grimsby Fishermen
Those who Catch the Fish
at the
ROYAL HOTEL
Tomorrow
Sunday Afternoon 23 March, 1890
At 4 o'clock

The same message was on hundreds of handbills which were distributed in the dock area of Grimsby on Saturday, 22 March. It was the idea of Samuel Plimsoll M.P. (1824-1898), the crusading 'sailors' friend', and Parliamentarian who persuaded Parliament to pass his controversial Load-line Bill in the Merchant Shipping Act of 1876. Controversial on the part of other M.P.s who were either shipowners themselves, or were closely concerned with shipping companies; and most probably share owners of these concerns, and who objected to his proposals on financial grounds.

Samuel Plimsoll had arranged to visit Grimsby after reading in the press the account of the supposed loss of the steam trawler *Sando* and her eventual finding and rescue by a relief vessel the *Sudero*. Plimsoll wanted to get right to the heart of the matter of just why so many vessels and fishermen were lost at sea.

A very large audience gathered at the Royal Hotel to see and hear the famous speaker, and supporter of the common seaman. Samuel Plimsoll began his lecture by saying he had come to Grimsby to see and talk to seamen and fishermen personally. Quite by chance he came at the time Grimsby was in a ferment at the imminent return of the trawler *Sando*, which had been given up for lost. The vessel was on her way home even as he was speaking. (Indeed she arrived in the port three days later on 26 March, 1890.) So one can imagine the great excitement as the news spread, and his audience, although a little in awe at their grand surroundings, would no doubt be more than a little lively. They certainly were when it came to question time at the end of the lecture

The speaker continued by saying he had, with some little assistance, tabulated a loss list of Grimsby seamen and fishermen for the months of January, February and early March, 1890. Some people, said Mr. Plimsoll, held the views that loss of both vessels and men was due to the incompetence of some of the men, and the shipmasters themselves. Yet if only each skipper could ship his own crew, this he felt convinced, would greatly remedy the situation. At the moment no captain had solely his own choice of men who were shipped under his command. Another point which interested his audience was the fact that all log books were kept ashore after each voyage, and this, said Plimsoll, ought not to be so. At certain times of the year also, irrespective of the weather being bad or not, skippers of fishing vessels were expected by their owners to bring back their catches to port within 14 days. If this was not done, owners were of the opinion that they were employing a poor skipper. The greatest loss of life amongst fishermen was when the transfer of the boxed fish was being made from the smack to the steam cutter which brought the boxes of fish back to port. This was a dangerous practice, and very risky work, done by the small ship's boat, often in very high seas. Samuel Plimsoll admitted that he knew very little about deep-sea fishing, but he asked if he could recommend the use of oil tanks on the cutter: the oil might be allowed to flow overboard in rough weather, and so prevent the waves from breaking, while the smack's boats transferred the fish. He said he knew that many American vessels carried oil-bags for this purpose, and the method was quite successful. He repeated once more that he was only an amateur, but could he suggest that the transferring of the catch by small boats might be dispensed with. Would not a strong net be sufficient to hold perhaps four boxes of fish? A net might be substituted and drawn to the cutter from the smack by a steam-powered winch. Unfortunately he overlooked the fact that some means of taking the net to each smack in the first place would have to be found, and this would mean a small boat being used, and so the whole scheme would fail.

Plimsoll was sure that many vessels were sent to sea by their owners in an unseaworthy condition, with complete disregard for the safety of the crew. At the time, he said, there was no test, or survey of vessels, no matter how old they were, and this should not be allowed to continue. In his closing remarks to the audience he said how he wished that all those who had opposed his Load-Line Bill in Parliament could have been with him in Grimsby to witness the joy and excitement in the knowledge that the trawler *Sando* was safe, when she had been given up for lost.

Concluding, Samuel Plimsoll stressed that it was no use the fishermen holding a Committee Meeting out on the Dogger Bank about their neglectful owners. What was wanted was some reliable men ashore, men who would look after their interests, and see that the Safety at Sea matters went ahead. Men who knew as much about the affairs as the fishermen and seamen themselves. Then Mr. James Alward, on behalf of the owners, said that 75% of skippers were not able to direct and instruct their own crews when at sea. The skippers were in command, but in many cases they were not competent to run a vessel. From then onwards, there were a great number of interruptions from the audience, and things began to get rather heated. One speaker in reply said he would like to see Mr. Alward, or indeed anyone else, go to sea with a set of men as they were sometimes compelled to do by the owners. Not long after this the meeting was brought to a close, but the insinuation by Mr. Alward brought a long letter in reply, which was printed in the *Grimsby News* towards the end of the month.

The letter began:

'I should like to tell the public I quite agree with Messrs J. and G. Alward that there are a lot of indifferent men holding certificates as Masters and Mates, but whose fault is it? Mr. G. Alward was one of the Examiners when these 75% of indifferent men passed for the Board of Trade certificate, and, if I remember rightly, Mr. J. Alward has a seat on the Smacks-men's Navigation Committee.

'So I for one think that they are themselves partly to blame for the said 75% of indifferent men they talk so much about. I fail to see how Mr. Alward can see his way clear to say that we lose 30% more hands than the codmen. If we compare the 700 trawlers with the 200 codmen (liners), then I think he will find they lose in excess of the trawlers. I fail to see why we should want more hands now, than in Messrs. Alward's time.*

'It appears that though we are compelled to have two certificates we are not such good seamen now as in their time. I can assure them that there are as good fishermen now, as then. I have no fear in saying, better, but it is an old saying that the Parson forgets when he was just the Clerk.

'Being at sea now, and 20 to 30 years ago, is quite different, In their time they went 50 or 60 miles offshore, if they went 100 miles, it was a mistake! Now we go 300 and 400 miles, where they never went in their lives. So surely we have advanced a little on those times . . . As for saying about the pipe of tobacco, and the pot of tea . . . I should like to say there is no sitting down in the cabin for 36 hours playing crick and keeping the deck boy up half the time. We may indulge in a little nap at times, but it is between sunset and sunrise, and, as the boy says, we do play fair.

'Maybe Messrs. Alward would give their comments on the fishermen of today when compared to those of his day?

I am, yours truly,
R. Wright
Smack *Kate Mudd*

No reply seems to have come from Messrs. Alward regarding these 'home truths', but James Alward did write and publish a series of long articles about the Grimsby fleet, which ran from early July until late in August, 1890.

*Note: The figure given in the letter from R. Wright appear to be at variance with the numbers of sailing trawlers and liners registered at Grimsby in 1889, as quoted from the Sixth Annual Report of the Inspectors of Sea Fisheries. The report gives the total numbers as 730 sailing fishing vessels. [See *Sea Fishing Apprentices of Grimsby* by David Boswell (1974).]

ENDYMION'S DAY

On completion of the *Narcissus* in 1887, Earle's Shipbuilding and Engineering Company Ltd., Hull, were successful in obtaining further orders from the Government, including machinery for several naval ships. Then in 1889 came an order for an armed first-class cruiser of 7,350 gross tons to be named *Endymion*. A little later the company were awarded the contract for a sister-ship to be called the *St. George*.

These orders meant an extension to the company's engine works which were not large enough to cope with the involved machinery, and the extensions themselves cost Earle's more than £8,000. The building of the new vessel was bedevilled with troubles, and a prolonged strike at Sheffield meant a late delivery of the armour plates. This and other difficulties delayed the completion schedule of the *Endymion* by many weeks.

However, on Wednesday, 22 July, 1891, the inhabitants of Hull shared a great occasion, which for more than a year after the event was invariably referred to as Endymion's Day by the workers at Earle's shipyard. This was the visit to the town by Lady Salisbury (wife of Lord Salisbury, the Prime Minister), who was accompanied by her son and daughter. The Honourable Lady certainly did her very best to visit as many places in Hull as possible, and while in the town she opened a hospital and launched a warship. She opened the new Victoria Children's Hospital in Park Street after a long delay in which the waiting crowds lined Park Street for hours, and everyone leaned forward expectantly as each

(Hull City Museums and Art Galleries)

Gateway arch at Earle's shipbuilding yard.

passing cab or carriage came down the street. They weathered three quite heavy showers of rain before the sun shone again and the official party appeared at long last, to declare the hospital building 'open'.

After the ceremonies Lord Hugh Cecil, the son of Lady Salisbury, remarked in his reply to the vote of thanks, that his mother had just performed a very pleasant duty, and later in the day she was going to assist in the launching of a ship, '. . . which would possibly be the cause of a great deal of suffering . . .' This was an unfortunate remark which was noted with some glee in the local newspaper; but then he was a young man with an unhappy knack of usually saying the wrong thing at the wrong moment!

An hour before the launch of the *Endymion* at Earle's, hundreds of people tried to crowd their way through the gates. From far away over the rooftops there could be seen the lines of coloured bunting, and flags flying from the cruiser, with one really huge Union Jack at the bow.

A maritime rule was the order of the day at Earle's. All visitors on entering the yard were confronted by two large boards, one on either side of the gateway, bearing the terms 'port' and 'starboard'. This was to guide the ticket holders, red tickets on the right, and green tickets on the left through the gateway arch. This mock-up archway of wood had been specially built for the occasion, and was painted to simulate stonework. There was a central arch over the main roadway with small turrets on each side. On the top beam over the central arch were small model vessels, also of wood, representing a cruiser and a merchant ships with crested shields over the two smaller side arches. Over the main roadway arch were jingoistic mottoes: 'Who commands the ships commands the seas', and 'Who commands the seas commands the world'. Both sides of the archway were alike, except that on entering the visitor read the words, 'Welcome to Earle's, and when leaving they saw over the inside of the arch the words 'Au Revoir'.

The lucky visitors were those who had tickets permitting them to mount the platforms around the *Endymion*'s bow, while the others had to be content to watch the proceedings from ground level. Even the privileged yard visitors had their troubles, for some were allocated seats on the platforms while others, though allowed by ticket on the platforms, were expected to remain standing during the proceedings. Inevitably, there were those with tickets to stand who had gone along early, and saw empty seats which they immediately occupied. Then there were the others who had tickets to sit, but found on arrival that their seats were taken by the first arrivals. After some polite struggles by the ladies, who urged their menfolk to remove the squatters, order was restored and the offenders encouraged to stand, but a general restlessness came over the waiting crowds who were growing impatient.

High over head, above the launching platforms towered the gilded and carved figurehead of *Endymion* who was portrayed in a reclining attitude, but ever watchful. All around on the special visitors' gallery platforms, were colourful military uniforms, tall silk hats, ladies' multicoloured dresses and decorated summer hats. Beyond could be seen the partially completed hull of the cruiser *St. George*, still building, but crowded with workmen, waiting to see the launch of the *Endymion*. The very centre of the main platform was reserved for really distinguished visitors who were to join the official party, and it was here that there stood the oak cabinet which contained the mechanism ready for the launching. It consisted of a mass of hanging ribbons outside and electric wires and levers inside.

At long last the official party arrived and mounted the platform. Sir G. Brown, Chairman of Earle's, and Mr. A. E. Seaton, the Managing Director, were presented to the Marchioness of Salisbury and the Lord Mayor of London. Mr. Seaton explained to her ladyship the intricate workings of the launching apparatus, but, before she could ask too many questions, she was hastily presented with a huge bouquet of flowers and an ornate pair of gold scissors for cutting the two ribbons which held the all important 'bottle'. The Bishop of Hull began the customary form of service beginning with the words '. . . All men that go down to the seas in ships . . .' and, when this was concluded, some time elapsed before word came that the workmen had completed the freeing of the two main cradles.

To pass away the time, further introductions and conversations took place between the distinguished visitor and members of the Board of Directors of Earle's. The Artillery Band played jaunty tunes to relieve the tedium, and a number of official photographs were taken by the press and by various studio photographers engaged for the occasion. This was long before the newspapers were able to publish actual photographs, and all the photographs had to be reduced by artists to line drawings to enable them to be used in newspapers. After what must have seemed like an age, a gold-coloured and decorated cord lowered itself, seemingly without human aid, from the high bows of the *Endymion*, and a quiet person then carefully fastened a large bottle of champagne on the end, and attached one of the official ribbons from the launch box, to the neck.

Lady Salisbury then gingerly cut the ribbon, but the bottle only swung gently through the air and bumped against the bow of the *Endymion*, not even cracking the bottle. There were startled glances, and one of the directors made a move forward, but the wife of the British Prime Minister was made of stern stuff, and a very determined woman. She looked at the advancing director, then, not wishing to lose her moment of power, she seized the still swinging bottle in a hearty grip and threw it against the bows of the warship. This time it really did smash with a fizzing frothy splash, and the Lady and the helpful director were flecked with large drops of golden champagne. At this instant the vessel began to creak and groan in its cradle that had held it secure for the past two years while building was complete. Slowly at first, but gathering speed, the great ship slid smoothly down the greased ways to the brown waters of the River Humber. The *Endymion* was well and truly launched.

The band was almost drowned by the cheers and shouts from an estimated 20,000 people there that day, After waiting for a few moments longer, Lady Salisbury and the official party then left Earle's yard for the Dock Offices where a dinner had been arranged to close the celebrations. Towards the close of the banquet, Mr. A. E. Seaton, proposing the toast 'Success to *H.M.S. Endymion* . . .', said that, 'Nothing in the building of the ship could have excelled the way in which her Ladyship dispatched the monster to the deep . . .!'

Not until 10.45 p.m. did the party leave the Dock Offices for yet another reception at the Town Hall, and even at that late hour, after a long and tiring day, Lady Salisbury was reported to be still enjoying herself. She really was a robust old lady!

(*Royal Naval Museum, Portsmouth*)

H.M.S. Endymion:
Edgar class cruiser; Earle's Yard No. 335.
360 ft. x 60 ft. x 31.2 ft. tonnage 7,350 gross.
Armaments: two 9.2 inch guns.
Ten 6-inch guns.
Four 18-inch torpedo tubes.
She saw worldwide service with the Royal Navy and served in the Mediterranean during the first World War as a training ship. Finally sold for scrap on 16 March, 1920, to T. E. Evans of Cardiff for £20,000.

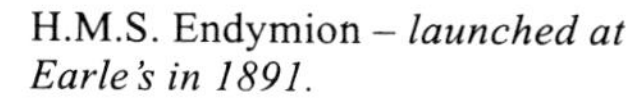

H.M.S. Endymion – *launched at Earle's in 1891.*

THE LAUNCHING OF THE CRUISER *ST. GEORGE*

The launch from Earle's Shipbuilding & Engineering Co.,Ltd., Hull shipyard of the cruiser *St. George*, a sister-ship to the *Endymion* which was christened by Lady Salisbury in July, 1891, was not marked by such formal recognition as in the previous year. Nevertheless, the occasion did attract a great interest in Hull, as the *St. George* was the last of the two first-class cruisers ordered from Earle's by the Government.

Lord George Hamilton, and Lady Hamilton who was to launch the vessel, arrived in Hull the day before the launch, which was due to take place on 23 June, 1892. The distinguished lady and gentleman stayed the night at West Hill House, Hessle, the home of Mr. F. B. Grotrian M.P.

The tides were not suitable for the launch until late in the afternoon of the 23rd, but soon after noon, crowds began making their way along Hedon Road towards Earle's shipyard. The entrance gates of the yard were decorated with flags, streamers and bunting; and large flags were blowing from staffs fixed on the *St. George* herself. The vessel was in a more advanced stage of completion than her sister-ship had been when she went down the ways the previous year. After the launch the new ship was to be towed round to Alexandra Dock to be fitted with her engines and boilers.

Long before the launch time of 4.30 p.m. all the vantage points of any value were occupied, and the Artillery Band, which had been engaged for the ceremony, helped to pass away the time by playing some military tunes to the assembled crowds. The weather, for June, was not of the best. The sky was dull and grey, and there was a hint of rain to come behind the massed banks of dark grey clouds.

The official party numbered well over 200, and their names took up 14 inches (35 cm.) of column space in the local press. This did not include a large number of Earle's shareholders who naturally insisted upon being present, but later complained when they found they had not been allocated seats with the official party, nor were they mentioned by name by the reporter for the local newspaper. This was just one of the headaches the management had to bear with on that day; there were a number of others. The Artillery Band continued to play cheerfully, although it was noted at the time they were more enthusiastic than accurate, for the band was obviously not in very good tune, due to some of its members partaking in a little pre-launch liquid refreshment! Lord George and Lady Hamilton arrived '. . . prior to the punctual moment,' as the reporter noted, about four minutes before their appointed time, and this again gave the management a certain amount of worry for they well knew the old saying about time and tide, and Victorian well-to-do people were not noted for arriving on time for functions.

Lady Hamilton had to be ushered forward immediately to the classic little oak-panelled box, with the weather-beaten figure of Lord Nelson on the top which contained the lever and wires to signal the actual launch moment to the workmen waiting below. The instructions were hurriedly explained to the lady, and then Mr. A. E. Seaton, a local J. P., stepped forward and presented the ornamental scissors to Lady Hamilton, with which she was to ceremoniously cut the silken ribbon. Unfortunately, his very short speech was completely inaudible as someone had omitted to inform the Artillery Bandmaster to cease playing. By the time the band were aware that the proceedings had begun, Mr. Seaton's words had been lost to posterity for all time. The gentleman was already seated again by the time the band and the spectators became quiet. Not a very auspicious beginning for the ceremony, and there were several frowning faces on the platform.

Red, white and blue ribbons fluttered bravely, and the champagne bottle was lowered from the bows of the *St. George* on a white silken cord adorned with fresh June roses just above the bottle, but, higher up, where the eyes of the viewers could not see the deception, the roses were all artificial! A rumour even went around, started by someone below the platform, that the champagne was not champagne at all but simply a cheap gooseberry wine. He was, justly, a wiser man later, when his coat was generously splashed by frothing champagne.

The usual official photographs of the launching party were taken, the men with top-hats raised, and the ladies' feathered hats fluttered in the strong breeze. An unlooked-for hazard this turned out to be when it was found that the ladies' decorated hats had blurred parts of the picture. After a short prayer by Canon McCormick, Lady Hamilton moved forward again and smilingly cut the ribbons. The champagne bottle made an arc outwards and cracked against the bows of the *St. George*. The cynic below was discomforted, although he stoutly maintained that one could not tell the 'quality' of the wine used for the occasion.

There came the sound of falling weights and a great creaking of beams as the bulk of the vessel began to move slowly down the ways. For a fraction of a moment she seemed to hesitate, then with another vibration she slid down towards the water. There was a sigh from the waiting crowds, shouts of, 'There she goes!', and a great noise of cheering from all parts of the shipyard. Without any further delay, the *St. George* glided serenely down the well-greased ways and rushed into the waters of the Humber. As her bows left the ways, it seemed she bowed to the crowds who had gathered to see the ceremony. It was a splendid finish.

Following the launch, the more important members of the official party adjourned by coaches to the Dock Offices for a banquet which had been arranged as a conclusion to the celebrations. A great display of indoor plants, potted ferns and cut flowers brightened the interior of the banquet hall. The long tables all had flower arrangements and silver candlesticks at intervals, and the ladies showed evident approval of all the arrangements, After the meal, Mr. F. B. Grotrian M.P. proposed the toast of 'The Army, Navy and Reserve Forces'. He then went on to speak for almost an hour. Eventually he ran out of steam, and only then did his audience begin to realise they had been listening, for a large part, to a campaign speech for the forthcoming elections! Nevertheless, they applauded enthusiastically and politely.

As the proceedings drew to a close, representatives from the management side of Earle's marked the ceremony by presenting Lady Hamilton with 'the handsome and pretty pair of scissors', which she had used earlier in the day to cut the launching ribbon. Lord George Hamilton had to be content with a small medallion in a plush-lined little case, but, then, his part in the proceedings had not been vary arduous!

The evening ended with a mention that, as one berth emptied in the shipyard, plans were being made to lay the keel of a twin-screw passenger steamer for the Great Eastern Railway Company. She was to be used on the Harwich-Continental run, and was to be 300 feet x 34 feet; of 4,500 h.p. making 17 knots and providing accommodation for 180 first-class and 60 second-class passengers. This vessel was the *Chelmsford* (Yard No. 367) and launched in 1893.

On this pleasant note the evening ended. The rain, which had held off all day to everyone's relief, began while the junketing was taking place in the Dock Offices. The happy revellers came out of the warm rooms, and descended the great staircase, to find the rain pouring down as they hurried into their waiting coaches. But the vessel was launched, and the meal had been splendid, so no-one minded very much; apart from the soaking wet coachmen, and the snorting stamping horses who were no doubt very glad to be moving homewards at long last.

St. George: (Yard No. 341) Edgar class cruiser.
Laid down 23 April, 1890: Launched 23 June, 1892
Engines by Maudsley: 387 ft. x 602.3 ft. x 231 ft.
Commissioned 25 September, 1894
Armament: 2 x 9.2 inch guns; 10 x 6 inch and 4 x 18 inch torpedo tubes (when built). She was the eighth ship to bear this name: the first was in 1622. She was converted to a destroyer depot ship at Chatham 1909-1910. In 1918 she was used as a submarine depot ship, where she remained until early in 1920 when she was paid-off. On 1 July, 1920, she was sold to Castle of Plymouth for scrap.

THE STRANDING AND LOSS OF THE GRIMSBY TRAWLER *CHILIAN*

The Grimsby steam trawler *Chilian*, a vessel of 161 tons, built by Edwards Bros. of North Shields for the Grimsby Fish & Box Carrying Company, was 115 feet in length and had a beam of 20 feet. She was powered by a 50 h.p. engine, and was launched two days before Christmas, 1893, by Miss E. Alward, daughter of G. L. Alward, the Chairman of the owning company.

The vessel arrived at Grimsby from her builders on Monday, 8 January, 1894, and 18 days later she left the port for river trials and compass adjustment. Several of the company directors, their wives and friends, had rashly asked if they could sail on the new vessel while she was undergoing trials. The trials were due to take place off the coast near Withernsea, and in the Estuary, but the weather gradually worsened after sailing, and a full gale was blowing by the time the Bull Light was sighted. The skipper had been pointing out the various buoys in the river to the official party, but by the time Spurn was reached, few were interested! One and all had only the same idea: how soon could they reach Grimsby and go ashore!

The *Chilian*'s trials were, therefore, curtailed by order of the directors, no doubt to the great relief of their very seasick guests, and, after rounding the Bull Light, the vessel returned to Grimsby.

The Skipper of the *Chilian* on her maiden voyage was to be Joseph W. Little, who formerly had been in command of the *Brazilian*. The *Chilian* was a remarkably successful vessel during her short career, and it was on Sunday, 8 April, 1894, while returning from the Icelandic fishing grounds, that she unaccountably ran ashore at full speed on the rocks off Filey Brigg. She had the dubious privilege of being one of the first screw-driven steam trawlers to be lost off the Yorkshire coast.

The weather was fine and clear as the *Chilian* left Icelandic waters, but thick fog had shrouded the Yorkshire coast for almost a week. The course was altered to South by West ½West shortly before she struck, and this proved to be her undoing, as events at the subsequent inquiry into her loss proved.

A few hours before the disaster, the ship ran into thin mist as she sailed south, and then dense fog-banks off the coast. The Mate called the Skipper, who said their course would take them eight or nine miles seaward of Flamborough Head. The log showed they had run 295 miles since passing Westray Firth, and the Skipper asked the Mate to take lead soundings when the log showed 300 miles.

The first sounding showed 29 fathoms, and shortly afterwards later soundings showed 28 fathoms, then 26 fathoms and shoaling. Only 20 minutes after the third cast of the lead, the *Chilian* struck violently full on to Filey Brigg. The shock threw everyone to the deck. The engines were run full astern, but the ship remained firmly on the rocks with her bows high while the flood tide rushed over her stern, and through the great hole gashed in her bows. Only moments afterwards, the inrush of water put out the stokehold fires.

It was obviously foolish even to contemplate launching the ship's boat in such weather amongst the dangerous rocks, but a number of the crew ignored the Skipper's orders, and crowded round the boat, trying to free her from the chocks. At this moment the *Chilian* lurched seaward, then slipped off the ledge of rocks into deeper water. Six of the crew were swept away and lost: the Chief Engineer, the cook, two trimmers and two deckhands. The Skipper, the Mate and three remaining crew members climbed into the rigging which still remained above the water, and they stayed there until 8 a.m. when the fog lifted, and they were seen and rescued by the trawler *Hercules*.

From the crew of 11, only five survived. No news of the disaster reached the shore until daylight, and, by the time rescue apparatus was moved to the Brigg, all the five men had been taken off the wreck by the *Hercules*. At the Court of Inquiry, held later, the Skipper said their compasses should have been true, as they had only recently been adjusted. He was using the bridge compass to navigate by, and it was possible he had not allowed sufficient deviation on a new instrument which may have been faulty.

The Mate told the Court how he and one of the crew had just left the bridge and gone below for a smoke. He then returned to the deck to take soundings, and after this he went and sat on a cask near the engine-room skylight, and was talking to the Chief Engineer who had come up on deck for a breath of air. The Chief had just asked if the vessel would reach Grimsby in the morning, when the ship struck the rocks. It was 3.30 a.m. After striking, the *Chilian* was slewed round by the waves until she was broadside on to Filey Brigg, and this was the cause of her slipping off the rocky ledge shortly afterwards.

The Mate recalled that he had shouted to the crew to put their life-jackets on and climb into the rigging, as it was useless to try and use the boat. The Skipper hung on to the whistle lanyard for as long as he dared, signalling for assistance, and to warn off the *Hercules* which was somewhere astern of them. He only released his hold on the rope to get his own life-jacket out of the bridge locker.

One of the surviving crew told how he was washed off his feet twice as he was trying to tie his life-jacket. Even before his life-jacket was securely tied, the trawler lurched to starboard and slipped off the rocks, and he was thrown into the sea. He was fortunate, and managed to catch hold of a rope ladder which was trailing over the side, where it had been washed by the sea. He pulled himself up the ladder, and then took to the rigging where he stayed until daylight. He saw that the fog was lifting, and soon made out the Filey bell-buoy about half a mile astern of the wreck. He stated in his evidence that he had never once heard the bell-buoy during the night, nor did he hear it ring at all, either before or after the ship was wrecked. This was the first mention of the Filey buoy, and the suspicion that it was not ringing at the time of the stranding of the *Chilian*. When the deck-hand was taken off the wreck by the trawler *Hercules*, they passed within thirty yards of the bell-buoy, and he said again that it was still not ringing then.

Skipper J. T. Little, returning to give further evidence, said he had been at sea for 22 years, and a skipper for 12 years. He had been the master of a steam-trawler for four years, and this had been his third year at the Icelandic grounds. He was very familiar with the course both to, and from, the Icelandic waters. His vessel was only ten-weeks old at the time of her loss, and he believed his compass must have been at fault, otherwise he could not account for the *Chilian* being so close to the land. He was convinced he was on a safe course at the time of the wreck.

John Jones, a third-hand, said he and some others had tried to launch the ship's boat, but a heavy sea swept the boat and his companions into the sea. As the wave carried him overboard, his arm caught the boom and some trailing ropes swirling about, he grabbed hold of the ropes and climbed higher out of the water into the rigging. When questioned further, he also claimed that he did not hear the Filey bell-buoy ringing. He said it should have been ringing constantly in such a heavy swell. The next witness to appear was William Eastham of Trinity House, stationed at Yarmouth. Regarding the Filey buoy, he said he had general instructions to visit the buoy whenever he was in the vicinity on routine patrol. He was asked if the buoy was out of position at the time the *Chilian* went ashore, as it had been found adrift no less than three times during the previous five months. Mr. Eastham admitted that he had found the buoy out of position on 30 November, 1889, when it had been dragged half a cable to the south south west and both the hammers on the bell were bent and locked. This was due, he thought, to the buoy being either run into by some unknown vessel, or to being struck by some form of heavy drifting wreckage. The former, was, he said, most likely. The buoy was repaired and returned to its correct position.

The Trinity House vessel visited the buoy again on 28 January, 1894, and once more it was found adrift, this time two cables length from its anchorage. The buoy was then securely moored on its station. On 21 February, and 11 April, 1894, further visits were made to the buoy, and on both occasions it was found correctly on station and in good working order. The Filey buoy, he concluded, was adequately anchored by two sinkers, one of 30 cwts. and the other of 20 cwts.; this latter visit was three days after the disaster to the *Chilian*, and all was secure.

In the course of the summing up, several points were enlarged upon. The *Chilian* had two compasses, one forward and the other on the bridge, and both were considered adequate and sufficiently reliable for the safe navigation of the vessel. Sufficient evidence had been given during the inquiry that both compasses had been adjusted on the trials, and again just prior to the fishing voyage on which the vessel was lost. Regarding the lifesaving apparatus, which was quite adequate: apart from the ship's boat on the foredeck, there were two life-buoys kept on the bridge, and sufficient life-jackets for each crew member. The jackets were kept in the men's bunks, which was standard practice.

The course alteration on 7 April was deemed neither safe nor proper, especially as the soundings taken with the lead-line were done with insufficient frequency when it was obvious land was nearby. The Court stated that the evidence given proved beyond doubt that the Filey Brigg buoy was secure, in position, and working at the time the vessel stranded. The *Chilian* was off course and too close inshore, and the ship would have been in imminent danger long before anyone on board could have expected to hear the bell-buoy.

Finally, the loss of the trawler was due to incorrect and faulty navigation on the part of her Master, a wrongful alteration of course, and the infrequent use of the sounding lead. The actual loss of life was due in part to those crew members who ignored instructions from the bridge, and the fact that in high seas, the vessel slipped off the ledge of rocks on to which she had stranded, while some of her crew were still endeavouring to launch the boat. The Master alone was in default, but the Court of Inquiry adopted a lenient course, and suspended the Skipper's certificate for a period of nine months. They did agree to grant him a second-hand's certificate during the time of his suspension.

The *Chilian* herself broke up and went to pieces in another gale the week following her stranding, She became a total loss, a regrettable tragedy for a fine new vessel.

THE LOSS OF THE *MOHEGAN*

One of the worst shipwrecks off the Cornish coast happened shortly after 7 p.m. on the evening of 14 October, 1898, when the liner *Mohegan* went on the rocks of the Outer Manacles at 13 knots.

The *Mohegan* was on her second outward voyage to America when she was lost. She was originally ordered by Thomas Wilson & Co of Hull, and she was built by Earle's Shipbuilding & Engineering Co in 1898. She was Yard No. 415, and was named *Cleopatra*, but was purchased, prior to her launching, by the Atlantic Transport Co. of London, for £140,000 in July 1898, and her name changed to *Mohegan*. Misfortune dogged the vessel even on the stocks. The prolonged national strike of engineers in 1897, delayed her construction for nine months, and she was barely completed on schedule. Work on the ship may well have been a little below standard, to meet the deadline, as there was a high penalty clause for nondelivery in the contract, which was not covered for the eventuality of strikes affecting the delivery date. As a result of this hasty completion, many leaks and other faults appeared during her initial crossing to America, which necessitated a dry docking in New York. On her arrival back in England, she was sent to a yard on the Tyne for a thorough overhaul.

The *Mohegan* was a very comfortable and well appointed ship for her time, she had cabins for 60 first class passengers, carried a crew of 97 and a number of cattle men to attend to the animals carried in pens on deck. She had four masts, with a single funnel amidships, and her maximum speed was 14 knots. Her length was 482 feet, beam 52 feet, and depth 35½ feet. She was built with eight watertight bulkheads, and steam pumps which could pump dry every compartment in turn. The enclosed bridge extended the full width of the ship, and reached back over the engine room. The music room, smoking room and all the state rooms were tastefully furnished and decorated in the best late-Victorian style, with much gilded woodwork and carvings of fruit and flowers.

The *Mohegan* sailed from Tilbury on 13 October, 1898, under the command of Captain Griffiths, with 53 passengers, 97 crew and seven cattlemen. Her mixed general cargo was very mixed indeed! The manifest listed over 3,000 ingots of tin, antimony and lead. There were church ornaments, a thousand boxes of artificial flowers, crates of china and plate glass, bales of carpets, cloth, boxes of gin, and empty glass jars. Boxes of travellers' samples, 200 boxes of lard, 10 crates of iron spindles, 55 sealed pails of dried prunes, 500 casks of creosote and 163 cases of tins of shellac. Also in the hold were numerous sacks of seed, rice and preserved ginger, together with barrels of tar.

On 14 October the vessel passed Prawle Point and signalled the coastguard station she wished her position to be reported to her owners. From the moment she passed Start Point, near Plymouth, she appeared to be off course, and far too close inshore. The coastguard at Coverack saw the lights of the *Mohegan* and realised she was far too close to the Manacle Rocks, and was heading for disaster. The Coverack coastguard tried to alert the lookout on the ship, by lighting blue flares and firing a rocket, but these were apparently not seen. The coastguard station alerted the lifeboat crew before the *Mohegan* had even struck the rocks, and but for this prompt action, many more would have lost their lives in the disaster.

On the liner the passengers were just about to begin the evening meal, and the young children were already in bed. One of the engineers who survived, described how at about 6.50 p.m. he felt a shock run through the ship, and then the bridge rang down 'stop engines'. Immediately, sea water began to pour into the engine-room so fast that within one minute he had to abandon his post and climb the ladders to the deck. The *Mohegan* had struck the Outer Manacles Rocks on the starboard side, tearing a great gash below the waterline and the sea came flooding into several compartments at once. Although the generators were placed well aft of the engine room, 14 feet of water put them out of action, making it impossible to work the pumps, and putting out every light in the ship.

In minutes the liner was three parts under water, with a 40° list to port. Captain Griffiths ordered the boats to be lowered, and was directing the passengers to their lifeboat stations as the fourth officer fired four distress rockets. The *Mohegan* listed over still further, rendering the boats on the starboard side completely useless. Without a light on board, the liner sank only ten minutes after she first struck the rocks. A number of lifeboats were still in the davits when she went down, and those who had managed to struggle up on deck had either to swim for their lives, or cling to the rigging, as the funnel and all four masts still remained above the water.

The lifeboat from Porthoustock was already on the way, and her crew burned white flares in the hope of attracting survivors and any boats that might have come from the wrecked liner. As the lifeboat reached the Outer Manacles, they rowed through large amounts of floating wreckage, and sighted one of the liner's boats bottom up with two men clinging to the keel. The men were taken off, and then cries were heard coming from underneath the upturned boat. The lifeboat's crew managed to pull out two women and a young child. The child was dead, but the two women were pulled to safety. One of the women later told how she had been at dinner when the liner struck the rocks, but had managed to scramble into one of the boats on the port side. She had no sooner seated herself than a large

(Hull Daily Mail)

Mohegan *wreckage on the Cornish shoreline.*

wave capsized the boat, throwing all survivors into the sea. She and another woman with a small child had been trapped beneath the upturned boat for over an hour, and during this time the child died.

The Porthoustock lifeboat continued on her rescue mission, and picked up more survivors from another boat which was almost waterlogged, and then the people clinging to the masts and rigging were taken aboard. One hundred and six people were drowned in the disaster, including her master, all the deck officers, a stowaway, and almost all the passengers.

The Atlantic Transport Co., the owners of the *Mohegan,* gave free passage to any relatives in America who wished to visit St. Keverne Church, where most of the victims were later buried in a mass grave in the churchyard, A number of bodies were embalmed and sent out to America, at the company's expense, and a memorial stained-glass window was put into the church. In the grassy churchyard, over the mass grave, fringed now with long grasses, is a stone cross bearing neither date nor epitaph, only the word *Mohegan*.

An inquiry into the loss of the liner was unable to reach a satisfactory verdict as to why the *Mohegan* was on a 'west by north' course, instead of 'west by south'. Neither the Captain nor any deck officer survived. Therefore, it was assumed that either the Master had given a wrong course, or the helmsman steered a wrong course after being given the correct one by the Captain. The loss of the *Mohegan* remained a mystery, as it does to this day.

Some three months later, a headless body was washed ashore in Caernarvon Bay, dressed in a captain's uniform with brass buttons bearing the initials A.T.L., and there seems little doubt that it was the body of Captain Griffiths, Master of the ill-fated liner. The *Mohegan* had been insured with Lloyds and other underwriters for £112,000, and salvage of her cargo began two days after she sank. The 3,000 ingots of tin were raised, and much of the antimony and lead, but little else. Within a week or so of the salvage attempt, the funnel stays gave way in a gale, and the funnel collapsed into the sea. After 18 months nothing of the liner was visible above the water.

No attempt was ever made to raise her, as the damage to her sides was so severe. After periodic salvage attempts to recover her engines and propeller finally succeeded after several failures, the hull of the wreck was partially dispersed by explosives. In 1904, six years after she sank, the ship's condenser was brought to the surface, but after this no further salvage on the *Mohegan* was attempted. Gradually, over the years, even her actual position was forgotten.

Early in the 1960's marine archaeology began to gain public interest, especially as aqualung diving gained popularity. Two diving clubs made several dives, searching for the wreck of the liner. Eventually, the wreck was located in 75 feet of water, and, since then, visiting divers to the area have explored the ship's remains thoroughly. The divers reported that almost the entire outer shell of the hull has fallen outward, and the large boilers stand up from their bed-plates surrounded by wreckage, and half covered in drifted sand and silt. Still visible aft of the boilers are the generators which failed when she struck, and left the liner without power for lights and pumps. A broken mast has fallen across a hatchway, and lies partly across a winch and a mooring bollard. Broken crockery and china lie scattered everywhere. Broken plates, cups and saucers, pots, bottles and jars lie all around. Only one single dinner plate has been recovered intact, still bearing the crest of her original owners, 'Thomas Wilson & Co. Hull'. The plate was presented to the Helston Museum by the diver who recovered it in the summer of 1966.

The ship's bell, still engraved *Cleopatra – Hull*, was found by a Coverack fisherman early this century, and he donated it to the maritime museum at Falmouth, a last link between Earle's shipyard and a Victorian liner, both of which have now vanished forever.

THE DOGGER BANK INCIDENT

At the corner of South Boulevard, and Hessle Road, Hull, there stands a grey statue of a fisherman wearing a sou'wester hat, a jersey and 'fearnought' trousers tucked into sea-boots. The statue was erected by public subscription to perpetuate the names of Skipper George Smith, Skipper Wheldon and Third Hand William Leggett. The memorial is a reminder of the night when a Russian Fleet ruthlessly shelled a defenceless group of fishing vessels, and then steamed away into the night, leaving dead and wounded fishermen and a sinking ship behind.

Shortly before midnight on Friday, 21 October, 1904, the Hull Gamecock trawling Fleet, which numbered almost 40 vessels, were trawling the then rich fishing grounds near Dogger Bank, some 200 miles from Spurn Point. At the time, Russia was at war with Japan, and the Russian Baltic naval fleet, comprising seven battleships, six cruisers, and a number of torpedo boats, was on its way to Port Arthur in the Far East when it passed the groups of trawlers in the darkness.

Suddenly, out of the half-light of the very early morning of 22 October, the trawlermen saw the steaming lights of the Russian Fleet. Almost immediately, the fishermen were dazzled by the glare from the Russian searchlights. The Russians pinpointed the trawlers with their searchlights, and for some reason they apparently mistook the Hull trawlers for Japanese torpedo boats. Without any warning, the Russian ships opened fire on the defenceless trawlers, and for 20 minutes the fishing fleet was bombarded by more than 300 shells.

Skipper George Smith, and Third Hand William Leggett of the trawler *Crane* were both killed instantly when their ship received the first and heaviest salvo. The Second Engineer of the *Crane*,

(Author's Collection)

Dogger Bank Incident – Moulmein *and* Mino. *Valentines of Dundee brought out a series of four 'Russian Outrage' post cards shortly after the event. This is No. 2 and possibly the best of the series. This card is postmarked 'Bath, 6 December, 1904'.*

(Memory Lane, Hull)

North Sea memorial, South Boulevard, Hull

although badly wounded in the chest, came on deck to give the alarm that the *Crane* had been severely hit below the waterline and was sinking. When attempts were made to launch the small boat, it was found that the boat was too badly damaged and was useless. Although the Mate was also injured, he seized a lamp and tried to signal nearby trawlers for assistance. The trawlers could not steam very fast, as they still had their trawls down. One trawler crew cut their own nets away, and sent up signal rockets to warn off the Russian fleet, but this merely attracted further fire on to the ship. The call for aid by the Mate of the *Crane* was seen by the trawler *Gull*, also owned, like the *Crane*, by Kelsall Brothers and Beeching. The *Gull* went alongside the sinking *Crane*, and transferred the two dead and seven injured to her own decks. The rest of the *Crane*'s crew were taken on board a cutter of the Missions to Deep Sea Fishermen, and within half an hour the badly damaged *Crane* filled and sank

(Memory Lane, Hull)

Russian Outrage – trawlers in St. Andrew's Dock, Hull.

(Hull City Museums and Art Galleries)

Memorial after the demolition of St. Barnabas Church, Hull.

stern first. The *Gull* herself was extensively damaged, and another vessel, the *Moulmein*, was hit by a shell which went clean through the galley.

The firing ceased as suddenly as it had begun, and the Russian Fleet steamed away into the darkness. Bewildered and shocked, the fishermen were left to search for lost shipmates amid the wreckage of shattered trawlers. Later, some of the wounded men were transferred to a hospital ship, and others less badly hurt were sent on board the *Moulmein*; both ships then sailed for Hull.

News travelled very slowly in the early years of the century, and the first rumours of the affair did not reach Hull until Sunday evening, 23 October. The incredulous fishing community at first dismissed the story as just a 'fish dock yarn', until the *Moulmein* arrived with the wounded, and the rumour was confirmed. Crowds gathered in the streets along Hessle Road. At every corner there were groups of

(Memory Lane, Hull)

Shell hole in the Moulmein.

people discussing the outrage. A special edition of the local paper was rushed on to the streets, and was sold out in a very short time. Those people with relatives in the fishing fleet hurried down to the docks, anxious for first-hand news. They learned the full story of the unprovoked attack, from Skipper Haimes of the *Moulmein*, and Skipper Whelpton of the *Mino*. The crowds watched grim-faced as the rest of the Gamecock Fleet steamed slowly into the Fish Dock, with funnels, companion ways and casings all bearing the jagged scars caused by the Russian shells, and with their decks littered with wreckage and shell splinters.

Feelings ran high in Hull when the full facts of the outrage became known. The indignation of the local community spread throughout the whole country. The Russian Embassy in London was stoned and several windows were broken after representations had been made to the Embassy, which brought forth nothing more than the usual expressions of regret and apologies. When the Russian Ambassador went to Victoria Station in London, he was hooted by a large crowd of enraged people who pressed forward showing their anger by waving clenched fists. A relief fund was opened in Hull for dependants of the fishermen who had been killed or wounded, and the list was headed by a donation of 200 guineas from the King and Queen.

A Board of Trade inquiry was held in Hull before Admiral Bridge, from 15-19 November, 1904. Many trawlermen were called upon to give evidence, and the inquiry was concluded in December, The Tzar had, meanwhile, expressed his regrets also for the incident, but the British Government demanded more than just an apology. The country wanted full compensation to be paid, and the Russian officers responsible to be put on trial.

At first Russia ignored all these demands, stating that the Russian officers had definitely seen Japanese torpedo craft amongst the Hull fishing fleet! This was why the Baltic Fleet had opened fire. The delay in satisfying the demands of the British Government brought the country to fever pitch, and for a few weeks it almost seemed that war with Russia was inevitable. The Channel and Mediterranean squadrons were ordered to sea, with instructions to detain all Russian naval vessels sighted – this in itself could have provoked war had any action commenced.

Then, unexpectedly, the Russians relented, agreeing to all the demands of the British Government; to recall their Baltic Fleet, submit the officers for trial, and pay compensation. The whole country breathed a sigh of relief. However, the officers never stood trial, and the Baltic Fleet was not recalled, but steamed on to its eventual destruction by the Japanese at the Battle of Tsu-Shima in May, 1905.

An international inquiry on the affair was held in Paris in January, 1905. After all the evidence had been heard, the Russian Imperial Government agreed to pay £65,000 in compensation. Henry Smirk, Chief Engineer of the *Gull,* was awarded the Albert Medal for courage in rescuing men from the sinking trawler *Crane*. William Smith, Mate of the *Crane,* was also awarded the Albert Medal for devotion to duty while his ship was sinking after being severely damaged by Russian gunfire. It is interesting to note that William Smith's Albert Medal was sold in June, 1971, at Sotheby's in London for £480. In 1905, part of the damaged companionway of the trawler *Mino* was presented to Major P. Malcolm D.S.O. Chief Constable of Hull. This companionway, with five shell holes through it, is on exhibition in the Town Docks Museum, Hull. The inscription on the small brass plate affixed to the relic, which gives details of the Dogger Bank Incident, is now worn almost illegible, after many years of polishing by museum staff.

All that remains to remind us of the affair is a worn and jagged section of black iron plate in the museum, and a grey statue standing on its plinth amid the busy traffic of Hessle Road, Hull.

A SEASCAPE – THE TRAWLER *CLYDE*

At the 1907 Royal Academy Summer Exhibition there was exhibited a dramatic oil painting by the well-known marine artist Thomas Somerscales, entitled *The Rescue*. The picture portrayed a Grimsby steam trawler in apparently high seas, alongside a sailing vessel in the North Sea, attempting to rescue her exhausted crew. This painting was later purchased, and generously presented to the County Borough of Grimsby, by Wilfred V. Doughty J.P. of Ickleford Manor, Hitchin. A photograph of this painting was the subject of a Christmas card in 1927 sent by Councillor L. K. Osmond and Mrs. Osmond to their close friends and relations.

This is the story behind the picture. On 6 September, 1906, the Grimsby steam trawler *Clyde* (built at Beverley in 1891 by Cochrane's, before their move to Selby), and under the command of Skipper George Freer, had left port and almost reached the fishing grounds in the North Sea, when the Mate, Christopher Bishop, sighted distress signals flying from a Russian barque. The strange vessel was the *Anna Mathilde*, out of Blyth with a cargo of coal bound for Riga. A strong gale was blowing and the sailing vessel was obviously in trouble as she was low in the water, and appeared in imminent danger of floundering.

Only one day out of Blyth, the *Anna Mathilde* had encountered heavy weather and sprung a leak. Her crew manned the pumps, but the water gained steadily. After more than 24 hours at the pumps, her crew were exhausted and could work no more, especially as coal dust from the cargo appeared to be partly choking the pump inlets. With her low freeboard, the high seas were continually sweeping aboard. The ship's lifeboat was smashed on her chocks and stove in, while almost all the lifebelts had been lost overboard. One of her crew was washed off the poop and thrown down to the main-deck, sustaining great injuries. Both his legs were broken, and one arm, and he had a severely fractured head. He was taken below by his shipmates and carefully placed in his bunk.

Shortly after this the trawler *Clyde* sighted the barque. Coming within hailing distance, Skipper Freer learned that the ship was likely to founder at any moment. In the tremendous seas, it was impossible to launch a boat, but with skilful management the skipper of the *Clyde* took his trawler alongside the disabled Russian ship. As he did so, one huge wave lifted the *Anna Mathilde* above the *Clyde*, and the sailing vessel's port quarter crashed down on the trawler's stern, which was crushed and badly twisted.

Another attempt was made, and the *Clyde* was put alongside. As both vessels grated together, the trawler's crew waited, ropes in hands. One by one, the Russian crew jumped from their vessel to the trawler's main-deck. The seven men who were on deck succeeded in jumping across without mishap as the two vessels closed. An eighth man grasped a line, but, as he did so, the trawler's bows suddenly dropped into the trough of a wave, and he was dragged from the barque's deck into the water between the two vessels. Fortunately, he kept hold of the line, and the trawler crew were able to drag him aboard, gasping and dripping wet, before the two ships smashed into each other again.

From the master of the *Anna Mathilde* it was learned that there was still one other crew member on board, the man who had been badly injured earlier. The *Clyde* stood by for several hours in the hope that the weather would moderate sufficiently for a boat to be launched to try and take off the injured man. Unfortunately, a little after 8 a.m. the barque, by then very low in the water, suddenly sank, on an even keel, carrying the injured man down with her.

The *Clyde* then put about, and returned to Grimsby, where she docked on Saturday, 23

September, 1906. A few weeks later, representatives from the owners, T. C. & F. Moss, held an official presentation to congratulate Skipper Freer and his crew on their part in the rescue of the Russian seamen. Skipper Freer was presented with an inscribed barometer, a medal and a purse containing £5, quite a large amount of money in those early days. A number of the crew of the *Clyde* were also given purses of £2 in recognition of their bravery. The following March, further awards were made on behalf of the Russian Imperial Government. Skipper Freer received a gold-plated chronometer, the Mate, Christopher Bishop, an award of £10, and each member of the crew of the *Clyde* was given £5.

Strangely enough, there was a sequel to this rescue only four years later. The *Clyde* was again in the news, this time under Skipper Herbert 'Joss' Mercer. In a force nine North Sea gale, through the rain squalls a three-masted schooner was sighted with a very severe list. The stranger was a Dutch vessel on her maiden voyage. During the storm, her cargo shifted, giving the ship a dangerous list. As the ship began to go over, her Master, who had his wife on board, became panic-stricken and, fearing that the ship was about to go right over, urged his wife into the small boat and abandoned the ship and his crew. In the heavy seas, the small boat was quickly swamped, and both the captain and his wife were lost.

The *Clyde* went alongside the schooner, and the Mate jumped aboard with a line. The frightened Dutch crew were encouraged by this, and a towline was hauled across and made fast. The steam-trawler towed the listing schooner the 240 miles back to Grimsby, where both arrived safely and moored in the dock. The owners received £800 as a salvage award some time later, and once again the trawler's crew benefited financially.

Clyde:
Built by Cochrane, Cooper & Schofield of Beverley (Yard No. 45) in 1891. Official No: 96247 ; Fishing No. G.Y. 317
Delivered by builders: 12 May, 1891
Owners: T. C. & F. Moss of Grimsby
97.2 ft. in length x 20.6 ft. breadth: 146 gross tons, 69 net.
The *Clyde* was in the same ownership until February, 1915, when she was requisitioned by the Royal Navy. She was fitted with a three-pounder gun and went on Auxiliary Patrol as FY 971 until she was lost in collision off Sidmouth on 14 October, 1917.

THE STRANDING AND LOSS OF THE *BERLIN*

There are a number of unusual circumstances which make the loss of the passenger steamer *Berlin* in 1907 a particularly sad affair.

The *Berlin* was built for the Great Eastern Railway Company's Harwich to Hook of Holland run (105 miles), by Earle's Shipbuilding & Engineering Co., of Hull in 1894. She was Yard No. 379: 302 feet x 36 feet, 1,745 tons gross. (A sister-ship, the *Amsterdam*, Yard No. 380 was built the same year.)

At the time of her loss the *Berlin* was under the command of Captain Precious who had been with the company for 31 years. The *Berlin* left Harwich at 10 p.m. on Wednesday, 20 February, 1907, At the time there had been severe weather conditions prevailing in the North Sea, with a great gale blowing from the north-west for several days. She made the crossing without any serious incident taking place, apart from the loss of some crockery in the dining rooms. The ship had endured the terrible gales, although many passengers had been ill in consequence. Yet the worst of the passage was over and only a mile and a half of water remained before the passengers could go ashore. In fact many of the passengers were on deck with their hand baggage when at the very entrance to the harbour disaster came suddenly and unexpectedly.

As the 5 a.m. bugle sounded to inform both passengers and crew it was almost 'going ashore time', the ship rolled as she was struck by a huge sea on her port quarter, swinging the bows to the northward. She came suddenly round as the wheel was spun out of the hands of the helmsman. A second sea caught her on the seaward side, and she was thrown broadside, with tremendous force on to the submerged toe of the North Pier, which was driven deep into the port side amidships. The vessel was momentarily impaled with her starboard side exposed to the full force of the North Sea gale, and great seas began to break over her.

An hour and a half later, the Railway Company's Agent in England received a message from the Hook of Holland which said '*Berlin* stranded on North Pier. Very dangerous. Heavy gale. Tugs and lifeboat going out to assist'. An hour afterwards, at 7.30 a.m., a second cable told the story – '*Berlin* a total loss with crew and passengers. Nobody saved.'

Desperate attempts were made to rescue those on board, but the toe of the pier, which tapered off under water, was a breakwater and support for a light tower which was constantly awash in rough weather. It was on this underwater obstacle that the *Berlin* had impaled herself, and in the huge breaking seas no vessel could get near the stranded ship. The local lifeboat got within ten yards of the wreck, but the recoiling seas beat her back, and all the boat could do was pick up bodies, and there were plenty, which had been washed from the deck of the *Berlin*.

By 7.20 a.m. the watchers on the shore saw that her masts were assuming diverging angles, and it was clear that the vessel had broken in two. After another 30 minutes of pounding by the high seas, it was seen through the squalls of rain and spray that the whole forepart of the *Berlin,* from just forward of the bridge, had broken clear away. Those still on this section were quickly overwhelmed and thrown into the water, either to drown or be washed and battered helplessly against the granite blocks of the pier. Huge waves broke

(Hull City Museums and Art Galleries)

Passenger steamer Berlin *(c.1906).*

with incessant regularity over the remaining stern and midships section of the *Berlin*, and high over her funnels. With each wave that crashed on board, more passengers or crew were washed into the foaming seas. Next to go was the whole of the bridge, together with the Captain and officers on duty.

The lifeboat remained just off the pier entrance hoping to find survivors, and at last one man was seen in the water, and he was picked up alive. He was Captain G. W. Parkinson, who was on the *Berlin* as a passenger for Amsterdam to rejoin his own ship. As he was washed overboard he managed to grab and keep hold of a section of timber, and luckily he was washed out to sea, away from the waves crashing against the pier. When he recovered sufficiently, he was able to give an account of what had happened to the ill-fated ship. He said he was in his cabin when he felt the ship strike. He hurriedly put on some clothes and went up to the bridge to tell Captain Precious who he was, and ask if he could give any help. Captain Precious had ordered the engines full astern in the hope of getting the *Berlin* off. But within minutes the engines stopped, and the Chief Engineer came rushing up to report the engine-room was fast flooding and that the incoming seas had put the fires out and they could do no more.

Captain Precious ordered his officers to instruct all passengers to put lifebelts on, and then he set about firing rockets and flares. He had little opportunity to say or do any more. The seas swept across the decks, smashing everything in the way. Within 30 minutes of the stranding, the ship's boats were pounded to pieces, then the bows broke away, to be quickly followed by the bridge and the Captain and officers. An hour after the *Berlin* was stranded, the cargo steamer *Clacton* arrived off the entrance of the harbour. Her crew tried to launch a boat to help the *Berlin*'s people but the violent seas prevented this. From the deck of the *Clacton*, the passengers on the *Berlin* could be seen huddled together, clinging to the twisted davits and rails, shouting for help as one after the other they lost their grip in the cold and were washed away by the breaking seas.

On the *Clacton* was J. W. Precious A.B., the son of the Master of the *Berlin*. All that day and the following night the gale continued, while rescue boats remained on standby, waiting for the first opportunity to make a rescue attempt. Not until after midday on 22 February did the sea moderate sufficiently to allow a boat's crew to land on the outer pier, which was no longer under water. From the iron framework of the light tower one man managed to seize the end of a boat's fall hanging from a davit down the side of what remained of the *Berlin*. Then a seaman from the *Berlin*'s crew was seen to slide down the fall into the lifeboat. His example was quickly followed by seven women, and the lifeboat returned with eight survivors from the wreck, and a report that there still remained three more women on the *Berlin* who were too exhausted with cold and fatigue to save themselves. Although the lifeboat attempted to reach the wreck, a rising tide and another gale made it impossible to get near, as waves began to break over the *Berlin* again.

But the three women were rescued. Captain M. Sperling of Dordrecht and three friends arranged for the owner of the tug *Wodan* to tow their flat bottomed yawl to the end of the pier. Captain Sperling moored his yawl to the beacon tower, and, although each wave battered his little ship, it was sheltered a little by the wreck. He climbed up the rope by which the previous rescues had been made, so becoming the first man to board the *Berlin* since she struck. He found the three women, still alive, but so utterly exhausted they could do nothing for themselves. One by one he carried them to the rail, and then tied ropes around them and lowered them to the pier. He tied each woman to the beacon posts while he went back for the others. Eventually he took all three to the yawl, and so back to the tug. The women were taken to the Hotel Amerika and given medical treatment, and after a few days they all recovered.

No further survivors were found, and, although the full death toll was never established, as the only records and passenger lists were lost with the ship, the Court of Inquiry found that 85 passengers and 48 crew had been lost, including the Master and all the officers. The survivors told how crew members had risked and lost their lives while venturing below to look for food for the passengers. One steward, C. E. Carter, the only crew survivor, said he and two others went below decks on such an errand, and his two companions were drowned as the pantry and companionway flooded.

When the tide went down and the storm moderated, the wreck was examined and it was found just how severe the seas had been. Waves had burst in all the cabin doors, and smashed all the interior furniture to pieces. The ship had been continuously pounded on the submerged toe of the pier, then waves smashed her against the sides of the granite pier, letting her fall back with her full weight on to the piles beneath her.

Great appreciation of the rescue attempts by the Dutch life-boatmen and Captain Sperling was made both in England and the Netherlands. Gold medals were presented to Captain Berckhout and Captain Jansen of the lifeboat and the tug, and to Captain Sperling. Silver medals were awarded to each member of the crews of the tug and lifeboat. Lloyds' of London also presented a silver medal to Captain Jansen and Captain Sperling. The final records of the Inquiry noted that the loss of the *Berlin* was due to an error of judgement on the part of her master in attempting to enter the narrow harbour entrance during a particularly heavy north-west gale, and failing to make sufficient allowance for the strength of the tide, wind and sea in so confined an entrance.

FOUR DAYS OUT . . .

This account of the first four days on the *Titanic* is based largely on some research into the experiences of Mr. Algernon Henry Barkworth J.P. of Tranby House, Heads Lane, Hessle, Hull, who was a first-class passenger on the *Titanic*, and Mr. Edmond Ryan, a family friend who went out third class.

The noon sailing time had arrived for the *Titanic* and the 'all visitors ashore' whistles and bells rang to warn non-passengers to leave the ship. Around 20 minutes later, the gangways were lifted clear and the mooring lines cast off.

So the last links with the shore were severed, and the ship with her attendant tugs slowly drew clear of the dockside. Then came the amazing incident with the *New York* when the wash from the *Titanic*'s huge propellers drew the *New York* from her moorings, snapping her lines. Tugs fussed between the two liners, and at last managed to re-moor the *New York*. The danger of collision so soon after the voyage began was averted. This incident so affected one passenger who watched from the boat deck of the *Titanic* that he left the ship at Cherbourg with only his hand baggage. His trunks marked 'Not wanted on Voyage' remained in the baggage hold, and are no doubt still there to this day. So he went ashore, and had a story to tell for the rest of his life.

Mr. Algernon H. Barkworth J.P. of Hessle, near Hull, was making the voyage as a first-class passenger. He was to visit friends in the United States and had originally planned to stay over for four weeks. He was one of the more fortunate passengers, being amongst those rescued, but in the light of unforeseen events he was required to remain in the States for longer than he intended due to the needs of the U.S. Inquiry into the loss of the *Titanic*.

The spring weather and fresh green leaves on the trees along Southampton Water caused many of the passengers to remain on deck in spite of the rather

(Hull Daily Mail)

Mr. Edmond Ryan, a Titanic *survivor.*

cool wind which was blowing. Cherbourg was reached at dusk on the Wednesday, and then the *Titanic* sailed, just before 9 p.m. after taking on European emigrants and mails.

The crossing to Ireland was made without further incident, and at Queenstown the last of the emigrant passengers came out by tender, Amongst them was 24-year-old Edmond Ryan from County Cork, going out to seek his fortune. He had his savings of £300 and the rest of his belongings in a rather battered leather case. He was hoping to get a job in New York as an engineer. He had no friends on board and was put into a cabin to share with two other, rather quarrelsome, men from County Sligo. One of his best remembered recollections was of being taken halfway down a tall ladder leading down into the engine room by a crew member he befriended. There, hanging on to the ladder rungs, he was amazed at the din and the noise from the huge engines which were driving the ship along at 22 knots. He was quite pleased to regain the deck and leave the noise and the heat to those better accustomed to them.We shall meet Mr. Ryan again later on.

With Ireland astern, the wind had become so cold that few passengers remained on deck to watch the land fade away, and the swooping attendant gulls finally departed as evening closed in. The First Class Lounge was filled with a smartly dressed crowd of smiling ladies and laughing men in evening dress. The huge ship still confused many of the passengers, and a number of the ladies stationed themselves at the top of the grand staircase, the better able to view the colourful throng standing around at the bottom of the stairway.

The strong smell of fresh varnish, polish and new paint contrasted strongly with the sea air of the decks outside. One or two of the ladies with weaker stomachs excused themselves and went to their cabins to lie down. The voyage proper had now begun, but few of the steamer chairs on deck were in use the next morning due to the extreme cold, and full advantage was taken of the cosiness of the Café Parisienne.

It was in the First Class Lounge that Algernon Barkworth made the acquaintance of two fellow passengers, also travelling alone. Their friendship quickly ripened, but lasted only four days. One was named Charles C. Jones. He was a farmer, going out to join his brother in Vermont. Young Jones was a Dorset man who had farmed in a small way, but he had sold his own farm and hoped to buy a section or two of land to become a partner with his brother. The other was named Arthur H. Gee. He was going out to become the manager of a linen mill near Mexico City.

They met each morning to talk to one another about their hobbies and ambitions, walking the deck on the lee side, dressed in warm coats. Mr. Barkworth felt especially warm and snug in his long fur coat: the same coat which in a strange way was to save his life three evenings later. Although it was April, and warm spring weather back home, by the second day the deck stewards had roped and lashed most of the steamer chairs in their vertical stowing positions. Indeed, so cold was the wind on deck that only a few hardy souls wrapped in rugs and coats remained reclining in the chairs. After about half an hour, the three companions agreed they had stoically endured the sea air for long enough on their promenade. By mutual consent, and with reddened cheeks, due to the wind, they went below to their cabins to leave their warm coats, promising to meet again in the First Class Lounge for a whisky and soda before lunch.

Mr. Barkworth's pet theme was the science of good road building. He was a Justice of the Peace, but had a great interest in civil engineering and never tired of telling his theories to whoever would listen. As he had a captive audience in his two new friends, they chaffed him about his hobby, as they smoked their cigars whilst sitting at the lounge table. While they ordered more drinks, he would take out an old envelope from his pocket book to draw them sketches, ignoring their smiles and exchanged winks.

So the days passed, with little intervals of interest such as when the competition for guessing the distance steamed took place, before the ship's daily run was posted outside the library entrance. The run from noon Thursday to noon Friday was only 386 miles due to docking delays at Cherbourg and Queenstown; but the Friday to Saturday run logged 546 miles, and then, perhaps due to the strong headwinds, only 519 miles from Saturday noon until midday Sunday.

The ship's library was well used, with numerous books out on loan, but none were read out on deck, the weather being now too cold. The comfortable library chairs were nearly all occupied by readers, while one or two of the more thoughtful passengers were writing letters home, or making up their diaries of the voyage. As to the letters, they could be posted in the little glass fronted mail-box at the entrance to the library. All the efforts of letter writing were to be vainly spent, and no-one gave a thought to them as the ship went down. No doubt what remains of the letters are still in the *Titanic*'s mail box at the bottom of the Atlantic.

So arrived the fatal Sunday, 14 April, 1912. The last meal was over, the very last meal for so many. Down in the Third Class Dining Room Edmond Ryan attended a rather noisy concert which made his head ache. He was glad to make his escape as the last song ended with cheers and stamping feet. He went below to his cabin where he found his cabin companions in a heated argument, Trying to quieten them down, he only succeeded in having them join forces against him for interfering! For the Barkworth trio, a final cigar in the First Class Lounge and a last drink before the three friends went to their respective cabins. They were still talking when they noticed a very slight jerk as when a ship nudges the jetty whilst going alongside. Some of the whisky in a full glass slopped over on to the table top, but otherwise there was no other sign as to what had happened. Below, it was a different state of events. The iceberg the ship had struck had sliced open a 300-foot section of the *Titanic*'s side.

Mr. Barkworth ventured to the door but the crisp cold night air made him duck inside and quickly close the door to the 'I says' of his friends. Mr. Barkworth admitted he was curious, and, leaving his friends finishing their cigars, he bade them goodnight and went below to his cabin to put on his long fur coat. As an afterthought, and he never could explain why, be picked up his life-jacket from the back of a chair, and took it up on deck with him, carrying it by the tapes. Under his left arm he also carried his dispatch case.

Within the hour, the majority of the passengers were out and about, hurrying to the lifeboat stations, as the ship was considerably down by the head. The three friends met once again, although neither Jones nor Gee had coats. Both had left it until too late to go below for warm clothing, and thought it unwise to venture down tilting stairways and to push down past the throng of upsurging people. Algernon Barkworth had learned to swim while at school at Eton, and he determined to try his luck in the water, as he realised all the boats had left the ship. Jones and Gee stood at the rails looking down at the dark water, the cold night breeze ruffling their hair as they shouted in each other's ears to make themselves heard above the roar of escaping steam. Suddenly, all was strangely silent as the steam ceased blowing off, and the screams and shouts of people took the place of the roar of the steam.

Algernon Barkworth did a strange thing. First he threw down his dispatch case with all his papers and valuables in it. He watched as it slid down the sloping wet deck and tumbled into the sea. Balancing with one leg straight and the other bent to compensate for the slope of the deck, he put his life-jacket between his legs, took off his long fur coat, stood on the hem, then tied his life-jacket around himself with the tapes. He then put his fur coat on again, buttoning it tightly over his life-jacket. So he prepared to quit the ship. He did not see his two friends again.

Howard Case, the Manager of Vacuum Oil Co. in London, watched his preparations. 'My dear fellow,' he advised, 'I wouldn't think of leaving the ship if I were you. Why, she'll float for a week,' and he calmly lit a cigarette. Algernon Barkworth was not reassured, and thought it was time to go. He felt it was unwise to dive in, due to the immense amount of floating steamer chairs and other objects. So he climbed over the rail until he was sitting on top with his feet outboard. Then he jumped feet first. His immediate sensation was the intense cold. The pain was rather like scalding. He went under but soon came up spitting out salt water. His fur coat buoyed him up like a bell, and he swam off towards a floating spar and a chair. He grabbed the chair, then, kicking his legs to keep warm, he made towards a lifeboat he could see not far away. As he drew nearer, he saw that the boat was capsized, but a little later the men on the upturned boat pulled him up out of the water. The boat turned out to be the Engelhardt collapsible boat 'B' in the charge of Harold Bride. Next day, after a night of unforgettable experiences, they were rescued by the *Carpathia*.

As to Edmond Ryan, he could not arouse his two companions from their bunks, as they seemed to be in a drunken sleep, so he left them to their fate. He lost all his possessions except his cherished pipe, but he managed to slide down a rope hanging over the stern into a lifeboat rowing beneath. He did not even get his feet wet!

Algernon H. Barkworth J.P. died at his home Tranby House, Hessle on 7 January, 1945, aged 80. He was ummarried and had no immediate family.

Edmond Ryan stayed in New York for three years, and then returned to England. In 1916 he moved to Hull to work for Rose, Downs & Thompson and later for Ideal Standard. He lived for many years in Welwyn Park Road and spent his final years in a retirement home in Pearson Park, where he died on 5 November, 1974, aged 86.

Mr. J. S. Boxhall, aged 28 at the time of the *Titanic* disaster, was the vessel's Fourth Officer. He lived for a time in Westbourne Avenue, Hull, and was an ex-Hull Trinity House Navigation School boy. He was at Trinity House School from 1898-1899 and then served on the *Cambrian Warrior* owned by W. Thomas & Co of Liverpool. He gained his extra Master's certificate in 1907 and then joined the White Star Line as a junior officer. His father, Captain Joseph Boxhall, was with the Wilson Line for a number of years.

Wallace Hartley, the ship's bandleader, was 34-years-old at the time of the sinking. He came from Dewsbury, and began his career as a bank clerk, but he had always been interested in music, left the bank and became a violinist at Harrogate Kursaal. Then for a while he toured with the Carl Rosa Opera Company. Attracted by the extra pay offered at sea for service on ocean liners, he made several voyages on various ships. Then he met the Musical Director for the White Star Line, who asked him if he would be interested in becoming the leader of the new orchestra being formed for the *Titanic*.

After he had signed the contract, he confessed to his father shortly before he sailed that he was not really keen to sail on such a large ship. He had already resolved to leave the sea in three months time as he intended to marry a local girl, a Miss Robinson, to whom he was engaged. Unfortunately, he and all the orchestra were lost when the *Titanic* went down.

UNLUCKY THIRTEENTH – *R.M.S. BAYARDO*

Disaster overtook the Wilson liner *Bayardo* on her thirteenth voyage, between Gothenburg and Hull, on 21 January, 1912. The vessel was constructed by Earle's Shipbuilding & Engineering Co. Ltd., of Hull, only being completed in June, 1911, and so was little more than six months old at the time of her loss.

The *Bayardo* left Gothenburg at 6 p.m. on Friday 19 January, 1912, with a crew of 44, 42 passengers and 1,800 tons of mixed general cargo. The weather had been very thick from leaving Sweden, and the fog became more dense off Spurn Point. The ship proceeded up the Humber with soundings being taken frequently as the channel narrowed.

A little before 7 a.m. on Sunday, 21 January, *R.M.S. Bayardo* ran aground on the Middle Sand almost opposite Alexandra Dock, still in thick fog. The ship glided on to the sandbank without any shock, but there she stuck, firmly held forward and amidships, leaving her stern clear of the bank and still afloat, and only a mere 20 feet from the deep water channel.

All the passengers were at an early breakfast as they expected to be going ashore by mid-morning. There was no panic as few of them were really aware of what had happened. Not until they were told to assemble on the saloon deck and prepare to leave the ship in lifeboats did the passengers realise the ship was in a dangerous position, which was expected to become even worse as the tide ebbed. All the passengers were sent off in three lifeboats, and then transferred to the tug *Presto*. But even then their worries were not over, as the *Presto* also ran aground on another sandbank! In the bitter cold of a January

(Hull City Museums and Art Galleries)

The Wilson liner Bayardo.

afternoon they had to wait two hours before the tug cleared the bank.

Efforts were made to free the *Bayardo* even before the fog lifted, but in vain. As the tide ebbed, the vessel began to strain; the first damage was in the engine-room, when the boiler water gauges and tubes burst. Plates along the deck began to buckle, and the stokehold plates were forced up. Next to go were the Marconi aerial wires, which strained and finally snapped with loud twanging noises like piano wires.

At low tide the ship was almost clear of the water, even her propellers being visible. As the strain became worse, due to the totally unsupported stern being almost out of the water, there were continuous noises as rivets gave way and flew out. Woodwork in the saloon panelling cracked and glass doors smashed. As the door frames were wrenched out of position, the doors themselves splintered from top to bottom. Strangely, electric bells were ringing continuously until the batteries were exhausted; this was due to some form of short circuiting.

The water was by this time several feet deep in the engine-room, and most of the fires had been extinguished. The engineers drew the fires that could be reached, and by evening, apart from her master, Captain Soulsby, most of the crew had left the ship and gone ashore.

The *Bayardo* lay nearer to the Lincolnshire side of the Humber than the Yorkshire shore. On Monday, 22 January, it was plainly obvious that her back was broken. She lay on an almost even keel, with her bows pointing towards Alexandra Dock, Hull, and almost dry at low water, but already silt was piling up and around one side to a depth of several feet. With the dead-weight of cargo she would not rise, and lay there, a pathetic looking object. At high tide, the ship had sunk so far into the silt that the only part of her superstructure which showed above water was the promenade deck and bridge.

A salvage expert reported that the position of the ship was extremely critical. The vessel was full of water and bearing heavily amidships. The shell plating had parted amidships on the saloon deck, and there was a three-quarter inch gap in the cracked and buckled side plates. The deck stringers had held, but many port-hole glasses were cracked. In the way of the break, all the decks were set up, and the wooden decks were started for a considerable distance on either side of the break line. Where the break in the hull occurred, on the line of greatest strain, the steel plating was badly corrugated for about nine frame spaces.

Joiners from the nearby shipyard of Earles', the yard that had built her, were sent out to strip the saloons and passengers' cabins etc., of the most valuable fittings and fixtures. All hope of salving the *Bayardo* herself was abandoned, as she had broken completely in two, with the forward section leaning at an angle, and filling up with mud, sand and silt with every tide, having sunk ten feet into the shoal.

The passengers' heavy baggage and trunks were rescued, and then attempts were made to reach some of the cargo. No steam was available and it was slow work with hand tackle. As the men worked they heard grinding noises as the ship 'worked' with the ebb and flow of the tides, and more plates buckled and gave way.

At low water, lighters were sent out to the wreck from Alexandra Dock in an attempt to salvage as much as possible of her cargo. Priority was given to bringing out some of the 2,800 casks of butter the vessel carried. Divers loosened the casks, which then floated to the surface and were loaded into the lighters. The valuable cargo of butter was still in good condition, as it was closely wrapped and packed tightly in the wooden casks. The workers from Earle's yard were busy over the next few weeks removing steam winches, davits, anchors and cables. Gradually, the *Bayardo* was reduced to a gutted shell. Much of her valuable cargo was successfully salved, including the butter, which was valued at £5 a cask. In the lower hold was a cargo of paper and pulp, and several tons of pig iron. But much of this had sunk beyond recovery into the shoals of the Humber.

The cargo Manifest was as follows:

2,803 casks butter	5,150 cases herring
943 rolls wood pulp	71 casks beer
217 rolls paper	172 packages paper
8 crates steel castings	60 boxes steel castings
201 tons pig iron	300 castings
2,280 bundles laths	2,660 bundles bar iron
9,883 pit props	2,046 bundles box boards
429 boxes nails	1,143 bales merchandise.

Many barrels of butter and cases of herring were washed ashore on the Lincolnshire coast, and some cases of herring were washed up at New Holland.

The master of the *Bayardo*, Captain Soulsby, had previously commanded the *Aaro* and the *Salino*, and was given command of the *Bayardo*, the pride of the Wilson fleet when the ship left Earle's yard in June, 1911. His feelings can be imagined as he was due to retire in the spring of 1912. The Wilson Line had no other vessel of equal size to replace the *Bayardo*, and so the *Spero*, which had been sailing from Grimsby, took the place of the lost ship on the Hull to Gothenburg run.

The official inquiry into the stranding and loss of the *Bayardo* was published on 2 March, 1912. The Court was told that the vessel had three compasses, one in the binnacle in the wheelhouse by which the courses were set and steered, another outside and in front of the bridge, which was used only for comparison, and a third aft which was not used at all. The two compasses on the bridge were in good order, and had last been adjusted on 25 July, 1911, by Castle & Co., Hull.

Lead soundings had been taken with care and frequency, but the Court concluded that the Master had not drawn from them such deductions as an experienced navigator of the Humber ought to have done. The findings of the Court were that the vessel should have anchored earlier until the fog cleared. The ship had not been navigated with proper and seaman-like care, and the stranding and loss of the *Bayardo* was caused by default of her Master, and he was severely censured.

Bayardo:
Constructed by Earle's Shipbuilding & Engineering Co., Ltd., Hull (1911).
Yard No: 576.
Owners: Wilson Sons & Co., Hull.
Dimensions: Length 331 ft., Breadth 47 ft., Gross Tonnage: 3,471.

Bayardo *on the Humber sandbank with her back broken (1912).*

(Hull City Museums and Art Galleries)

THE *SARGON* – AN EPIC OF THE TWENTIES

On 2 March, 1923, the Standard Steam Fishing Company of Grimsby received a very strange cable from Reykjavik, Iceland. The full text of the cable was as follows:

> '*Sargon* towed in by trawler *Schleswig Holstein* of Geestemunde today, March 2nd. *Sargon* without coal. Burnt all gear, and crew without food except fish for sixteen days. *Sargon* picked up off Ingoldsfolde. Towed about two hundred miles. *Sargon* now requires 70 tons coal, small boat, provisions and engine-room stores.
> Signed Agent, Reykjavik.'

The Grimsby trawler *Sargon* with a crew of twelve under Skipper J. McCarthy left her home port on 5 January,1923, bound for the fishing grounds off the Murmansk coast and White Sea. They had hardly reached Spurn before a full gale was blowing, and, after only one day out, they encountered another trawler, the *Ethel Nutten* of Granton, flying signals of distress. She was a steel trawler of 182 gross tons, built in 1906 by Hall, Russell of Aberden, and owned by the firm of T. L. Devlin.

The *Sargon*'s crew managed to get a towline across, and they commenced to tow her towards the Scottish coast. During the voyage the towline parted and one of the *Sargon*'s deck-hands, H. Beavers, was injured by the flying end of the hawser. With difficulty, the line was reconnected and the tow continued. Unfortunately, after towing the *Ethel Nutten* for more than 80 miles, it was clear she was about to founder, and all her crew were taken off before the ship went down.

The shipwrecked crew of the *Ethel Nutten* were landed at Leith, and while in port, the *Sargon*'s injured deck-hand was also put ashore for hospital treatment. In place of the injured man, a young

(David Buckley Collection, Fleetwood)

Grimsby trawler Sargon.

Granton fisherman, John B. Bell, was signed on as crew replacement. It is interesting to note that young John Bell had been a member of the lost *Ethel Nutten*'s crew.

After leaving Leith, the *Sargon* had a very rough passage across the North Sea in a strong force nine gale. The vessel steamed around North Cape and appears to have been rather close in to the Russian coast off Murmansk, for she was sighted by a Russian patrol ship who gave chase. There were numerous incidents in the Twenties, of trawlers being challenged and arrested off the Russian coast for alleged poaching inside territórial waters. In a number of cases the trawler crews were jailed for several weeks prior to a trial, and eventual release, to return home thin and wasted after their imprisonment. Fortunately, the *Sargon* eluded the Russian gunboat in the short winter daylight, and managed to escape in the gathering darkness, reaching safe fishing grounds on 20 January.

After an uneventful spell of fishing she hauled her nets for the last time and sailed for home. This was in the days before fishing vessels were equipped with radio, and the *Sargon* put into Harstad, Norway, for coal and fresh water, and to cable her owners and notify them the vessel was homeward bound. They left the Lofoten Islands on 3 February, and should have been back in Grimsby four or five days later, but nothing further was heard from her. The *Sargon* and all her crew appeared to have vanished somewhere in the North Sea.

The weeks passed, and on 20 February the vessel was officially listed by her owners, as 'lost with all hands'. The *Sargon* was insured with the Lincolnshire Steam Trawling Mutual Insurance Co., and financial compensation was paid by them to the wives and relatives of the lost crew. The Shipwrecked Mariners' Society also responded by paying £53. 10s. (£53.50) to the crew's relatives, although only two of the crew were members of the Society.

Eleven days later the cable came from Reykjavik, with the news that the *Sargon* and her crew were safe in an Icelandic port.

The astounding news was received by the owners, the Standard Steam Fishing Company, and representatives said they could hardly believe it at first. Within half an hour a clerk was sent out in a

Crew of the Sargon *after their return to Grimsby.*

(Humberside County Council Leisure Services Department)

specially hired taxicab to call at the homes of the Skipper and crew, and give the relatives the amazing news. Apart from the cable that the ship was safe, nothing further was known until the trawler returned to Grimsby.

Mrs. McCarthy, the wife of the *Sargon*'s Skipper, and Mrs. Challis, wife of a deckhand, who both lived at the same address, were the first to hear that the *Sargon* and her crew were safe. The brother-in-law of Mrs. Challis had also heard the news at the owners' dockside office, and rushed off to take the good news to the two ladies. Strangely, Mrs. Challis was the sister of H. Beavers, the injured man who had been landed in Leith at the beginning of the voyage. Both ladies somehow could not really believe that the ship was lost, and yet both had sent some of their clothes to be dyed black. On hearing the news, they were both concerned to know if their mourning orders could be cancelled.

The wife of the Third Hand, W. Thomas, was also an early one to hear the good tidings, and she went straight to a telephone to have the news confirmed by the owners. She, too, said she had not believed her husband was lost. Although many wives had gone into mourning she was one of the few who did not, being convinced the ship was still afloat, and the crew safe.

After leaving the Lofoten Islands, the *Sargon* ran into more heavy weather and gales which swiftly increased to hurricane force. The ship was compelled to reduce to half speed, and for three days she battled against the weather without making any progress whatever.

It was soon clear that the Harstad coal remaining in her bunkers, which was soft Belgian coal and burned at a terrific rate, would be insufficient to allow the vessel to reach Grimsby. Skipper McCarthy was compelled to order all spare timber to be sent below as fuel for the engine-room boilers. Pound boards, bobbins, spare nets and even the nets from the steel warps were cut up and bundled into manageable armfuls to be thrown under the boilers. In spite of this, the coal was soon used up and the pound boards vanished in smoke. The *Sargon* began to drift helplessly north-westwards into the north Atlantic, and, being without radio, she was unable to send out a call for help.

Another worry was the shortage of provisions, and the food was all consumed by 11 February. Fortunately, they had ample fresh water, and supplies of fish down below in the fish-room. The crew lived almost exclusively on their catch, cooked in a variety of ingenious ways: fried fish, smoked fish, wind-dried fish, boiled fish and fish soup. Towards the end of their drift they had to chip wood from the bulwarks to feed the stove, and some of the wood chippings were used to smoke fish fillets which had been wind-dried on the bridge top. Attempts were made with lures, and even a few seagulls were caught to vary the diet of eternal fish. This shows how desperate the men were, but it was only a very reluctant and half-hearted attempt, as all trawlermen are superstitious, and look upon the gulls as reincarnated fishermen.

The steady and monotonous diet of fish brought on an outbreak of dysentery, but this was treated fairly successfully by Skipper J. McCarthy with the help of the ship's medicine chest.

Drift ice was sighted on 26 February as the *Sargon* drifted closer to the coast of Iceland. The following day she was sighted by the German trawler *Schleswig Holstein*, and in answer to the Grimsby vessel's distress signals she altered course. The crew of the *Sargon* launched their small boat, and a few of the hungry men manned the oars to make two crossings to the German ship for provisions. Unfortunately, a wave caught the boat on the second return trip, and the weak crew were unable to prevent it from being smashed against the *Sargon*'s side. The provisions were hurriedly thrown up on decks and the crew quickly scrambled aboard, but the boat sank and was lost. After a diet of fish for the previous 16 days, fresh food was more than welcome. The German ship took the disabled trawler in tow towards Iceland, more than 200 miles away, where both vessels arrived on 2 March at Reykjavik, and a cable was sent immediately to the owners telling of the safe arrival of the *Sargon*.

The *Sargon* was coaled and partly re-provisioned in Reykjavik, and, after putting into Aberdeen for more coal, reached Grimsby safely on the evening tide of 10 March,1923. She had been away for 65 days.

Every vessel in Grimsby with steam up joyfully sounded their whistles and sirens to greet the returned ship. Huge crowds gathered in Riby Square, and at the dock entrance. So many tried to push through the gates that the police and authorities were compelled reluctantly to allow only close relatives and near friends to enter the dock estate and go aboard the moored *Sargon*.

As Skipper McCarthy and his crew left the docks they were given a huge reception by the cheering, shouting, waving crowds, and Skipper McCarthy was carried shoulder high across Riby Square. The Skipper was very modest regarding his part in bringing the trawler back to her home port. 'A greater captain than I was in command of the *Sargon* . . .' he said.

It was rather ironic that a German trawler should have been responsible for saving the *Sargon*. For in those early days of the Twenties, all German trawlers were banned from landing a catch in Grimsby, an aftermath from the Great War, which had ended only a little more than four years earlier.

As for the *Sargon*, she was lost with all hands many years later.

THE HULL FISH DOCK FIRE OF 1929

The sun was low in the sky on a fine summer Sunday evening in late August, 1929. The day had been clear and sunny when shortly after 7 p.m. on 25 August Mr. J. W. Charlton, a fish dock worker who was walking along the dockside of St. Andrew's Dock, Hull, noticed clouds of grey smoke rising lazily over the new landing sheds and offices. Smoke, which even as he looked, turned to a red glow, and flames burst through the roof while the smoke rose higher into the still evening air.

As Mr. Charlton ran to raise the alarm he saw two dock policemen, a sergeant and a constable, and they telephoned for assistance. The Hull Fire Brigade lost no time in sending three engines to the scene of the fire. So quickly did the brigade turn out that at one point there was almost a serious accident on Anlaby Road, at the old Cecil cinema corner, when one engine nearly overturned while taking the corner at speed.

The fire spread rapidly along the rooftops of the sheds and offices. By 8 p.m. only an hour after the outbreak was discovered, the fire reached its greatest height and was visible for many miles around. By then there was no possibility of saving the range of buildings, and all that could be done was to keep the fire contained.

Dense clouds of thick black smoke billowed into the clear evening sky and the flames themselves were more than 50 feet high. The whole length of the new timber extension and fish merchants offices was a mass of roaring flames. Hundreds of people living on Hessle Road went down to the bottom of Liverpool Street and up on to the overhead road bridge to watch the spectacle. For some time there was a great fear that the fire might endanger other buildings along the dock. At that time, the London & North Eastern Railway distributed much of the fish landed in Hull, and three trains consisting of hundreds of wooden

(Hull City Museums and Art Galleries)

The Hull Fish Dock fire of 1929.

fish wagons were standing in the sidings, close by the blazing sheds. Many of the wagons were saved by the firemen playing their hoses on them until a team of shunters managed to raise steam in some engines and move the further wagons to safety.

The heat was terrific and many wagons were already alight and beyond saving. Another handicap was the many hoses lying across the tracks, causing a number of railway wagons to be abandoned. More than 100 wagons were shunted to safety, but 105 were completely destroyed in the fire.

All the combined efforts of the Hull and L.N.E.R. brigades were of no avail in putting out the fire, which began midway along the half-mile of new fish-market landing sheds and merchants' offices. From the centre, the fire roared both ways along the timber roof. One great source of trouble to the firemen was that their efforts were hampered by the flaring of gas mains and explosions as the gas meters blew up. The gas was responsible for the quick spreading of the fire, and not until almost 9 p.m. did an engineer manage to cut off the gas at the mains and so stop the supply.

The huge clouds of black smoke and flames were seen from the Lincolnshire side of the River Humber. At New Holland and Barrow, which were almost directly opposite the fish docks, the explosions could be heard distinctly on the still evening air. The impression at first was that the fire extended for a considerable distance behind the docks, and that many houses in the city were affected. Fortunately, this was not so.

The new fish market extension had taken a year and a half to build, and was almost completely of timber, apart from the supporting steel girders in the sides and roof. The work was completed only two days before the fire destroyed it in a little over four hours.

The new building was 468 yards long, the ground floor contained large quantities of wooden fish boxes, kits, new gear for discharging trawlers, and weighing machines and ice chests. The first floor had suites of fish merchants' offices, complete with new furniture and fittings. A balcony ran the whole length from end to end, with intermediate stairways for access. At the rear of the offices were store rooms, full of new stock, fish-boxes and kits etc. All the offices, like the rest of the building, were built of timber, with steel girders and wooden floors. The whole of this great building together with the offices and stores was completely destroyed.

As the building blazed, and the fish wagons were set alight by the terrific heat, there was great concern about the seven trawlers which had arrived on the morning tide, and were moored waiting to discharge their catches on the Monday.

In spite of all the rescue attempts, three trawlers were completely burnt out by the spreading flames. These were the *Lord Deramore, Ohm* and *Marconi*. The watchman of the *Lord Deramore* at first refused to leave his vessel, but the thick smoke became almost unbearable, and he put on a life-belt ready to jump into the dock. He was later taken off by a tug.

Due to the energetic efforts of the dock workers who turned out to help, two tugs, *Biddy* and *Ingric,* were manned, and a number of the burning vessels were towed to the far side of the dock. The trawlers saved were the *Norman* (135 net tons), owned by Hellyer Bros., and built in 1911; *Dairycoates* (141 net tons), owned by City Steam Fishing Co., built at Selby in 1926; *Frobisher* (131 net tons) owned by Hudson Bros., built in 1920; and *St. Alexandra* (156 net tons) owned by Thomas Hamling & Co., Ltd., built at Beverley only the year before, in 1928.

The heat was terrible, and at the height of the fire it was impossible to approach nearer than fifty yards of the burning buildings.

Once the burning trawlers were towed to the south side of the dock, the firemen were able to concentrate on these vessels and extinguish the fires on board, for most of these vessels were well alight, with masts, decking, bridge and boats all burning. Four of the trawlers were saved from too severe damage, but not before the catches were completely ruined. All the moored trawlers had watchmen on board, and all but one were taken off by one of the tugs. The watchman on the *Dairycoates* was cutting the mooring lines when he fell overboard between his vessel and the blazing landing quay. A young teenager rowed a small boat across the dock and rescued him, although he was reported to have said later he felt 'half scorched and half drowned'.

Four other boys went on board the *Frobisher* before she caught fire and took off the ship's cat which was below in the galley. One man was injured on the *St. Alexandra* when the burning rigging gave way, and a dan-buoy which was tied in the rigging fell to the deck, and knocked the watchman down. He said afterwards that he felt no pain at the time and carried on with the rescue work. Not until sometime later did he collapse, and he had to be assisted on to an improvised stretcher to be taken to the medical station further along the dock. He was then taken by ambulance to the Hull Royal Infirmary in Prospect Street, where he remained for a few days.

Dock workers were responsible for saving the *St. Alexandra,* which was well alight. They climbed aboard and chopped through the mooring lines, pushed the vessel from the burning jetty with their feet; she then drifted to the other side of the dock and the waiting firemen. Decks and masts were all blazing but this was one of the trawlers saved, though badly damaged. The watchman on the *Dairycoates*, despite having a wooden leg, remained on board his vessel cutting mooring ropes until she drifted into the middle of the dock. He then jumped into the water and swam to a painter's raft, from where he was later rescued.

By daylight, when the fire was finally extinguished, the full extent of the damage became apparent, and it was realised that the Hull fishing industry had suffered a severe setback. Smoke-begrimed firemen and dock-workers stood in groups looking at the still glowing embers which steamed and smoked into the pearl-pink sky of the Monday morning dawn.

The half-mile-long building with 98 offices and their contents valued at £100,000 was completely destroyed. Of the seven trawlers and their catches of 200 tons of prime fish, which had been moored to the landing quay, three were completely burnt out and four badly damaged, while all the fish in their holds was rendered useless. Three fish trains of 105 wagons were also destroyed. The total destruction of buildings, offices, stores, railway wagons and the damage done to the trawlers was estimated as being in the region of £250,000.

Hundreds of wooden fish barrels and kits had been thrown into the dock to save them from the fire, and, before they could be used again by the fish merchants, the barrels had to be pulled from the dock and well scrubbed, as the dock itself was covered in a floating skin of burned timber and other scorched materials. The newly installed patent fish landing gear had been destroyed in the fire and this meant that all the condemned catches in the partly burned vessels had to be unloaded by hand. Fresh fish from the North Sea trawlers, which docked on the Monday's tide, was landed first, and the merchants somehow managed to pool sufficient supplies of boxes for packing purposes. Almost all the day's orders were met, although supplies of deep water fish were in short supply. Box and barrel makers found all their available stock in great demand, and orders for new boxes came pouring in from merchants who had lost their entire stores.

Fish prices rose considerably in the local trade, due mainly to the fact that, as quay landing space was at a premium, a number of trawlers were directed to Grimsby and other east coast ports. The few vessels which came to Hull on the Monday's tide, some from Faroe and others from the North Sea, had their catches landed, but the owners decided to leave the Icelandic trawlers' catches on board the vessels, as the fish would keep better in the fish-rooms due to lack of landing and storage facilities.

The cause of the fire was never really established. The buildings were lit by electricity, although gas was also laid on for heating and other purposes. Some thought a faulty fuse was to blame. Others were of the opinion that the hot summer sun was the cause, shining through the glass skylights into upper rooms full of inflammable materials.

Within a month or so, with amazing cheerfulness, work began to clear away the burned-out ruins, and rebuild the landing sheds and merchants' offices.

Details of the burned-out trawlers, all of which were either repaired or completely rebuilt:

Lord Deramore:
Built in 1928 by Cochrane & Sons Ltd.,Selby.
Yard No. 1026.
Owners Pickering & Haldane Ltd.
Fishing No. H.461
140.3 ft. long x 24 ft. breadth.
134 net tons, 346 gross tons.
Repaired after the fire, reported as 'Lost' 6 March,1933.
Foundered returning from White Sea fishing grounds.

Ohm:
Built in 1915 by Cochrane & Sons Ltd., Selby.
Yard No. 627
Originally *Welbeck* for Letten Bros., of Grimsby.
Sold to F. & T. Ross Ltd. in 1920. Renamed *Ohm* (18 June).
Sold to Westward Trawlers Ltd., in April, 1946, and renamed *Westcar*.
Fishing No. H128. Official No. 137020.
135 ft. long x 23.5 breadth.
128 net tons, 302 gross tons.
Scrapped July, 1960.

Marconi
Built in 1916 by Cochrane & Sons Ltd., Selby.
Yard No. 656.
Owners: R. & T. Ross Ltd.
Fishing No. H488. Official No. 139288.
136.2 ft. long x 24 ft. breadth.
131 net tons 322 gross tons.
Reported 'Lost' 20 September, 1941, in collision off Harwich.

Dairycoates
Built in 1926 by Cochrane & Sons Ltd, Selby.
Yard No. 988.
Owners: City Steam Fishing Co. Ltd. (Delivered 4 January, 1926).
Fishing No, H270. Official No. 149046.
140.3 ft. long x 24 ft. breadth.
141 net tons, 350 gross tons.
On 25 May, 1939, purchased by Royal Navy and renamed *Quannet*.
Early in 1946 she was sold to Dutch owners and renamed *Klaas Wyker*.
She was sold for scrap in 1958

Frobisher
Built in 1920 at Goole.
Owners in October, 1923, were Hudson Bros (Trawlers) Ltd.
Fishing No. H170
138.3 ft. long x 23.7 ft. breadth.
131 net tons, 323 gross tons.
She was noted as 'sold' on 6 July, 1931.
Originally ordered as *Benjamin Hawkins* (Mersey Class).
W.W.1 Completed 7 February, 1920 as *Frobisher*.
In April, 1933, she was re-purchased by Royal Navy and renamed *Fastnet*.
On 20 February, 1942, she was transferred to the Dutch Navy, and in April, 1942, was abandoned off Batavia.

Norman
Built in 1911 by Cook, Welton & Gemmel Ltd.
Yard No. 212.
Owners: Imperial Steam Fishing Co Ltd. (Registered in Hull, 4 May, 1911).
Fishing No. H249. Official No. 132241.
140 ft. long x 24 ft. breadth.
135 net tons, 346 gross tons.
Sold to Hellyer Bros. Ltd., in October, 1919.
She had steam steering fitted in August, 1922, and was renamed *Dervish*.
Requisitioned by the *Royal Navy* in June, 1940, she was lost when she struck a mine off the Humber on 9 September, 1940.

St. Alexandra
Built in 1928 by Cook, Welton & Gemmell Ltd.
Yard No. 490.
Owners: Thos Hamling Ltd.
Fishing No. H373. Official No. 160093
140 ft. long x 24 ft. breadth.
156 net tons, 339 gross tons.
On 11 March, 1939, she was sold to the Royal Navy and renamed *Larch*. After the war ended she was sold to St. Andrew's Steam Fishing Co. Ltd., in November, 1947, and renamed *Westhill*.
Fishing No. H470.
On 15 September, 1950, she was transferred to J. Marr & Son Ltd.
Finally in October, 1952, she was sold for scrap to British Iron & Steel Corporation.

SHOAL WATER – THE *EDGAR WALLACE*

Hull has had its share of disasters to trawlers of the fishing industry. As each winter approached, there was always the fear that the sea would claim yet another victim in Arctic waters. Each ship lost is a grim tragedy, but perhaps one of the saddest of all was the loss of the Hull trawler *Edgar Wallace* on 9 January, 1935, when 15 out of a crew of 18 perished in the cold waters of the River Humber, almost within sight of their own homes.

Because of fog, the *Edgar Wallace* was three days overdue from a 21-day trip to Bear Island. The fog had cleared 48 hours earlier, but the moonless January night was very dark. The Humber was full of shipping, and the navigation lights of other vessels could be seen as moving points of light in the darkness. The voyage was very nearly over, and most of the crew of the *Edgar Wallace* who were off-duty were below decks, or in the fo'c'sle collecting the last of their gear together, ready to go ashore in a little over an hour.

The trawler was slightly to the westward of St. Andrew's Dock, near Hessle Sands, with a fast tide running. One moment the vessel was steaming up river at half speed, a minute later the bow went on to the sand bank and was held fast. The Skipper appears to have kept the engines going ahead, in the hope that the ship would clear the bank. Unfortunately, this did not happen. The engines pushed the bows still further on to the shoal, and the stern moved past the bank in a 90° turn, bringing the vessel broadside on to the tide. There was a slight jerk, then the force of the swiftly flowing tide turned the ship right over. The stokehold fires were flooded, and the lights went out, leaving the ship in total darkness. Only three crew members survived, the cook, Clarence Wilcocksen, and two spare hands, W. Cameron and C. Hendrick.

Cameron had managed to squeeze through a porthole as the *Edgar Wallace* turned over on her side. He was found clinging to the foremast, and was rescued by men from the *William Cass*. A second man who was with Cameron, clinging to the mast, became exhausted and slipped off and was lost. Cameron said later that in the dim light he saw seven or eight men swept away by the swiftly flowing tide and lost to sight in the darkness. Although they cried out, nothing could be done to save them.

One of the first vessels to arrive on the scene was the *Ernrix*, under the command of Captain H. Cowling. A boat was launched to help in the rescue operations, as many shouts and cries could be heard coming from men drowning in the dark water. Unfortunately, the small boat started to fill with water, and the three men in it had to put back to their own vessel and climb on board to save themselves.

Another survivor, Clarence Wilcocksen, the cook, together with two other crewmen, managed to climb along the rigging which was almost horizontal. His two companions were washed off the rigging and not seen again. Wilcocksen found a lifebelt still lashed to the rails, and this saved his life. He was in the cold water for almost an hour and a half before he was picked up by the steamer *Goole*, and he was later landed at Goole.

Hendrick, the third survivor, was found by the crew of the *Angularity*, very nearly unconscious from cold and exposure, clinging to a pound-board. He had held on to the rigging with one arm, but with his body in the icy water. He became so cold he lost all sense of feeling, and had to release his hold. As he was swept clear of the ship, a pound-board struck against his neck. He grabbed the board, and held on to it with a rigid grip. When dawn broke, six rescue vessels were still standing by, but there was little to be seen of the floundered trawler. Due to the turn of the tide and currents, the vessel had returned to an even keel on the bed of the river, but only the top of the funnel and the two masts showed above the muddy waters of the Humber.

On the dockside, workers and relatives of the crew stood waiting, crowded round the offices of the owners, the Newington Steam Trawling Company, as the list of the missing crew members was pinned up on the notice board. The quiet cold of the grey January morning was broken by the cries and weeping from the girls and women in the crowd. Later in the morning, a tug steamed slowly up river towing a marker buoy which was moored near the lost vessel. Another trawler, coming out of the St. Andrew's lock-pit, bound for the fishing grounds, nosed out into the Humber, while many of her crew stood on deck in silent tribute to friends who had been lost from the *Edgar Wallace*.

Among the missing, were the Skipper, Mate and Chief Engineer. The Skipper, J. Stevenson, who was only 32-years-old, left a wife and one child. The Mate, Edward Gibbons, was 27 and single. The Chief Engineer, J. Malony, left a wife and five children. Others of the lost crew included 21-year-old Robert Thornton who was making his first trip on a trawler, and John Desmond, also 21, who had only recently started going to sea.

Salvage work on the sunken vessel was started within a day or so. At low water, the masts, funnel and bridge top were showing, but already the ship had began to sink into the fast-holding mud shoals of the Humber. During salvage operations, James Vessey from Gainsborough, a crew member of the Hull tug *Boatman,* was lost overboard. The *Boatman* was assisting in the salvage operations when the tug fouled a lighter and capsized. Three of the tug's crew were able to swim to the lighter, and climb on board, but James Vessey was swept away by the tide and drowned.

Salvage proved very difficult and hazardous, and after a week or so all hope of raising the *Edgar Wallace* was abandoned. The unlucky vessel was eventually blown up to clear the channel, as she had become a serious danger to navigation.

The tug *Boatman* was built by Cochrane's of Selby, being Yard No. 1006; 57 feet x 14.2 feet and 31 tons gross. She was delivered on 24 April, 1927, and reputedly cost £1,750.

Edgar Wallace:
Built in 1925 by Cochrane & Sons of Selby.
Yard No. 987:
Owners: Newington Steam Trawling Co. Ltd.
Delivered: 18 December, 1925
Fishing No: H262. Official No: 149042
140.3 ft. long x 24 ft. breadth.
138 net tons, 336 gross tons.

THE LOSS OF THE *LADY JEANETTE*

During the late afternoon, on a grey and very windy March day in 1939, the Hull trawler *Lady Jeanette* was steaming up the Humber after a 15-day trip to the fishing grounds off the Norwegian coast, with more than 1,300 kits below in the fishroom. Spray was blowing across the decks and most of the crew were already changed into their shore-clothes, and were off watch below playing cards. The young cook, who was only 18, was in his galley washing up and clearing away the tea-stained mugs and large tea kettle after the last brew of the voyage.

On the bridge Skipper G. Parkinson was alone with the Mate, E. Fell, who was at the wheel. Orders were then given to the Bo's'n to anchor a little east of the St. Andrew's Dock entrance. It was at this very moment when the anchor touched the bottom of the river that a faulty shackle parted the anchor cable. Immediately, the high winds and strong tide drifted the *Lady Jeanette* on to a sandbank. Quickly the vessel began to heel over. The Mate let down one of the bridge windows and shouted to the crew to stay on the ship, because, as soon as the trawler began to heel over, the men came scrambling up from below. The Skipper clung on to the siren lanyard and gave five short blasts; this was his last action before the tilt of the wheelhouse deck flung him off his feet.

The Bo's'n and three spare hands had left the whaleback anchor winch as soon as the vessel began to tilt over, and had hurriedly made their way along the sloping deck, and up the angled ladder to the boat deck. Here, in the few minutes left they tried to launch the small boat, but the boat was still fast to the davits when the trawler heeled over to the same side with a jerk which threw the three spare hands off the boat deck and into the swiftly flowing muddy waters of the Humber. The three men were swept away and not seen again.

Once more the Skipper and Mate shouted from the bridge windows to order the crew to stay aboard the ship and hang on to the ladders or mast stays.

Both the Skipper and Mate then made an attempt to get out of the wheelhouse by scrambling up the steeply sloping decking towards the door at the highest side. As the Mate reached the door it slammed shut, trapping his fingers. Fortunately, he managed to force his way out, and he climbed on to the side of the bridge in time to help the Skipper who was able to climb through one of the bridge windows. A number of the crew, including the cook, either did not hear, or misunderstood the order to stand by the ship, and they jumped over the side, intending to swim for the shore. But once they were in the water they were lost. The tides run extremely swiftly thereabouts and they too, were swept away.

The Master of the Humber ferry *Wingfield Castle* saw the disaster as his vessel was crossing to New Holland, and altered course to try and aid the stricken ship. Unfortunately, the state of the tide made it virtually impossible to approach the wreck without endangering the lives of the passengers on board. As other vessels were nearing the scene, the ferryboat continued on her way to New Holland.

The first rescue craft to reach the scene was a tug coming from Goole and a power barge *Cité de Paris* which was on passage from the Lincolnshire side of the River. They found men clinging to the sides of the trawler, and at great risk the tug went close in to try and take the men off. Strong winds were sending spray flying high over the wreck, and, as the *Wingfield Castle* had been seen near the submerged vessel, it was thought at first that a number of the *Lady Jeanette*'s crew had been taken off by the ferry and were to be landed at New Holland.

The trawler was by then right over on her starboard side, and the tug found it difficult to get very close in. The power barge was smaller and the Skipper, Mate and seven of the trawler's crew managed to get on board, while the tugmen hauled the Bo's'n from the boat-deck where he was still clinging to the rails.

The tug *Triune* and the barge *Cité de Paris* then made for the St. Andrew's Dock entrance to land the survivors. Without hats, many without jackets, and the Mate with his injured hand roughly bandaged, the rescued crew wearily made their way to the Insurance Building for medical attention.

Large crowds quickly gathered outside the Mutual Insurance and Protection Building where a list of those saved was hurriedly posted on the noticeboard. Nine of the crew were missing and presumed lost, although there was hope for a time that some might have been picked up by the ferry-boat, but in an hour or so this was regretfully announced as untrue.

Relatives of the crew, including many women,

The Lady Jeanette

(David Buckley Collection, Fleetwood)

(Hull City Museums and Art Galleries)

Low tide, the day after the disaster to the Lady Jeanette *(1939).*

thronged the doors of the Insurance Building, waiting for news. One of the women refused to be kept outside in suspense. She pushed and elbowed her way up the stairs to the room where the roll-call was being taken, and the men were being issued with spare, dry clothes.

'Where's our Stan?' she demanded of the officials. Unfortunately, they could not answer, for her son, 19-year-old Stanley Harvey, was one of those missing.

By early morning on the 9 March, the day after the disaster, the *Lady Jeanette* had almost righted herself, due to the turn of the tide, but only the masts, funnel, bridge top and part of the fo'c'sle whaleback were above water at low tide.

The tugs *Waterman* and *Motorman* went out with officials to see what were the possibilities of salvage. Hopes of salvage were quite high, and four days later it was reported that a German salvage company had been engaged to refloat the *Lady Jeanette*.

Within 26 hours of the loss of the *Lady Jeanette*, two other trawlers, the *St. Delphine* and the *Aquamarine,* were in collision in the Humber, and the *St. Delphine* sank with the loss of three lives. The same German salvage concern was also engaged to try and lift the *St. Delphine* after the *Lady Jeanette* had been salved.

These early months of 1939 were momentous times, and the attempts to raise the *Lady Jeanette* were squeezed off the front pages of the local newspaper by large headlines such as 'German troops massing', 'Prague occupied' and 'Hitler takes Slovakia under his protection'. So it can be understood that local feelings were strongly against a German company being asked to undertake the salvage work. In fact one local M.P. asked a question in Parliament. He wanted the President of the Board of Trade to say why a German salvage company had been called in to lift the *Lady Jeanette*, to the exclusion of tenders from British firms.

However, Messrs. Bugsier of Hamburg sent the tug *Mowe* and two super lifting lighters, the *Willie* and the *Kraft*, equipped with special lifting tackle and steel hawsers.

Crowds watched from the St. Andrew's quayside as preliminary surveys of the area were made, with the assistance of local tugs.

After a wait of several days for favourable tides, the last days of March saw the *Lady Jeanette* moved 100 yards from the hole that had been scoured around her sunken hull by the wash of the tides. Special eight-inch pliable steel cables had been swept under the hull of the trawler until she was resting in a cradle of wires. The lifting craft slowly winched the cables in at low tide, then, as the tide turned, the lighters were lifted, the *Lady Jeanette* stirred and was slowly lifted clear of the riverbed. Little of this final work could be seen by the watchers on the dockside due to haze on the river.

Once clear of the river mud, the bulk of the *Lady Jeanette* was winched to the surface until all the superstructure was clear and the decks just awash. The German salvage crew connected up the pumps and pushed armoured hoses and pipes through every deck opening in an attempt to clear the trawler of water and large quantities of river mud and silt which had accumulated inside the hull. This was one of the reasons why the salvage was unsuccessful, as the German equipment was unable to cope with the thick silt, and the pumps quickly choked.

More than 40 tides had passed over the *Lady Jeanette* since she sank, and now that she was at the surface the ravages of the Humber could be clearly seen. There was a deep dent along her starboard side where the whole weight of the vessel had rested on the mud-bank. The mainmast was bent and the rails on the starboard quarter had vanished completely, cut away by the lifting hawsers. Thick mud was everywhere, and the trawl-net, normally stowed along the starboard rail, had broken adrift and was trailing across the deck and tangled in the hauling winch.

By the 11 April, more than a month after she went down, the *Lady Jeanette* was still only a mere 100 yards from where she sank. Strong tides had impeded the work of lifting her, and, although the support wires were still in position, the pumps had been unable to clear the mud and silt from inside the hull, and she had been allowed to settle on the bottom once again to await more favourable conditions.

Knowledgeable local inhabitants had said that salvage would be impossible, and by 15 April they were proved correct. Salvage attempts to raise the *Lady Jeanette* were abandoned, and after more than a month's work the German salvage concern admitted defeat. Between lifting attempts, the strong tides of the Humber had tangled the lifting wires under the hull of the trawler, which had sunk 14 feet into a mud shoal. A large bank of mud had formed along the sunken vessel's starboard side, and another shoal had accumulated off the port bow, making it impossible for the lighters to get close alongside to make a successful lift. Moving the *Lady Jeanette* any further was impossible, and so, with a month's work wasted, the lifting wires were unshackled from one lighter and winched up by the second one.

The German salvage tug and the lighters then moved down river to attempt to raise the *St. Delphine*.

Attempted raising of the Lady Jeanette

(Memory Lane, Hull)

Hull trawler St. Delphine *(c.1930).*

(David Buckley Collection, Fleetwood)

At the end of April the news headlines stated that Hitler still hoped for '. . . an understanding with England', 'there was no cause for War . . . but . . .'And in Hull the Air Raid sirens were tested for the first time on 1 May.

Two days later there was a rather gruesome find on the Humber bank near Immingham. A human head was discovered on an offshore mud bank. The decomposed head was injured as if it had been struck by a ship's propeller; and it was thought to be one of the victims of the trawler disasters in March.

On 12 May the German salvors also abandoned their attempts to raise the trawler *St. Delphine*. They collected their gear together, and, with the lighters in tow, the German tug departed for Hamburg. It seemed that with war clouds looming the salvage attempt was only half-hearted, and the company was anxious to return to Germany while it was still possible to do so.

On 11, 12 and 13 May a Board of Trade Inquiry was held on the loss of the *Lady Jeanette*. Skipper Parkinson related how the loss of the vessel had been caused by the parting of the anchor cable. The Mate and several members of the crew were also questioned. The Skipper was 30-years-old at the time and came from a seafaring family in which there were no fewer than five trawler skippers. He had held his ticket for four years prior to the loss of his command.

In announcing its findings, the Court stated that the trawler should have anchored further down the river, clear of any possible mud shoals. They suspended Skipper Parkinson for 12 months, but recommended that after six months he could be granted a Second Hand's certificate if he so wished. This finding so enraged Skipper Parkinson that he threw down his certificate on the table, walked out of the room and left the building.

With all the salvage attempts on the *Lady Jeanette* abandoned, the only recourse left to clear the channel of the obstruction was to disperse the wreck with explosives. The task of dispersing the wreck of the *Lady Jeanette* was given to the Lincoln & Hull Water Co., at the end of September, 1939, and work began in the first week of October.

Previous efforts using explosives had been withheld due to the War situation, but it became imperative to clear the wreck for navigation purposes. The public were warned by the local press not to be alarmed at the sounds they might hear coming from the river, which would take the form of very heavy rumblings. Final work in clearing both wrecks ended in the last week of October, 1939. The *Lady Jeanette* was only two-years-old at the time of her loss, while the *St. Delphine* had been in commission for just over 11 years.

Lady Jeanette:
Built in 1937 by Cook, Welton & Gemmell Ltd., of Beverley, Yard No. 616.
Owners: Jutland Amalgamated Trawlers Ltd.
Launched: 20 March, 1937. Completed 1 May, 1937.
Fishing No: H466. Official No: 165658.
162 ft. long x 27 ft. breadth.
471 gross tons

St. Delphine:
Built in 1927 by Cook, Welton & Gemmell Ltd., of Beverley. Yard No. 491.
Owners: Thomas Hamling & Co Ltd.
Launched: 31 December 1927. Completed 12 January, 1928.
Fishing No: H380. Official No: 160096.
140 ft. long x 24 ft. breadth.
358 gross tons.

TRAWLER COOK – *STELLA ARCTURUS*

It was one of those wet, rainy afternoons in early spring. Too wet and unpleasant to be out of doors when it wasn't really necessary. I decided it was a good opportunity to tidy up the loft. Climbing the ladder into the cavernous roof space, I heard the rain drumming on the tiles overhead. I began to re-arrange things and in about 15 minutes I had managed to make one corner look much tidier. I moved a carton containing several odd rolls of wallpaper, and revealed an old kitbag. A kitbag with fancy knotwork handles of crown-knots, wall-knots and other knots whose names I have long since forgotten.

Immediately, I was back in time more than 40 years, to a July day in 1952 . . .

The trawler owner's small shipping office was crowded that warm summer afternoon, the air acrid with the blue haze of strong tobacco smoke. The crew of the trawler *Stella Arcturus* had just signed on. Meeting them for the first time they were, to me, just a blur of strange unfamiliar faces.

One person, though, made a lasting impression. He was a little below average height, inclined to be stocky, but with a jolly face and an infectious laugh. His fair hair was receding slightly above bushy eyebrows but one thing took my eyes right away from his face. This was a huge 'kipper' style tie, with a large picture of a well-built girl in a minuscule swimsuit; hand-painted I found out later. I was also informed he had a collection of about a dozen of these ties, all featuring different young ladies, and all in the briefest of swimsuits. His firm handshake gripped mine. He confided that he was the ship's cook and would be my best friend on board, especially when I was hungry. He invited me to visit him in the galley whenever I felt like a snack.

This was my introduction to Steve Roberts (not his real name by the way, but it will suffice). He was then 43 years old. He had been a P.O. in the Royal Navy until 1946, and had served in the Merchant Navy before joining the trawling fleet as a cook.

The Skipper of the *Stella Arcturus* was his father-in-

(Memory Lane, Hull)

Hull trawler Stella Arcturus.

law, but they didn't get along very well together, and rarely a voyage passed without an 'incident' of some sort between them. The rest of the crew couldn't understand why he didn't ship out with another firm of trawler owners, but he wouldn't take any advice on this subject, much to the crew's surprise.

Working in the hot cramped galley was no place for fancy ties, and I was not to see Steve wearing one of his ties again until the day we docked. It invariably brought a smile to one's face to see him calling the first sitting to the mess-deck each meal time. Steve kept an empty beer-crate under the galley sink, which had two uses. It was either to sit on when he peeled potatoes, or to stand on when he poked his head out of the galley skylight on the boat-deck each meal time. 'Aho-o-o-y!'he would roar, nothing more. His voice would penetrate above a gale, even down in the fish-room. Everyone knew this meant the meal was ready, and those off watch usually needed no further urging to hurry into the mess deck. Steve would be waiting in the galley, to pass the stew, or pies, or a mass of fried fish through the serving hatch, to whoever arrived first. 'Dig in!' he would say, or, 'Fill your boots, eat hearty but rapid!' His stock phrase never varied each meal time.

During one afternoon, while we were still steaming to the fishing grounds, I tried my hand at fancy rope-work, knotting and splicing. Steve Roberts, the cook, was my instructor. It was really his watch below. The weather was fine but becoming cold, so we sat together on upturned fish baskets, on the engine-room casing, near the funnel. We were out of the wind, and it was pleasantly warm leaning against the funnel. Steve showed me how to begin a lanyard for my kitbag, using four different types of knots, working with twine 'borrowed' from the net store without the Mate's knowledge.

We spent two pleasant hours working together, and then he had to return to his galley to brew up the 4 o'clock cocoa. I put the lanyard aside for another time, and went off to find a mug for some hot cocoa.

An evening or so later, I had to do a little 'make and mend' on my smock which I'd torn on a ragged steel stanchion in the fish-room. The cook lent me his 'housewife' (case of needles and thread) to do the job. By the time I had finished it was quite late, about 11 p.m., but I stopped on in the cabin a little while watching the cook playing cards with 'Darkie' Johnson, one of the engineers. Then I turned in.

Passing the galley one afternoon on my way to the fishroom to stow and shelve cod, the cook asked if I would take the Skipper's allocation of sugar up on the bridge, to save him a journey. Knowing how things were between him and our skipper, I agreed. 'Have you seen the "motto" hanging in the wheelhouse?' he asked me. As a matter of fact I had, but I said I would make a point of having a look. I don't know where it originated, but it will bear repeating, as it typifies the modern trawlermen.

The 'motto' was burned on a plain varnished piece of wood, probably with the end of a hot soldering iron. The verses read:

'Good luck to all you undertake,
Never worry, never break,
Play your best, the game's worth while.
Win or lose, play on and smile,
And sportsman-like in all you do –
Be never beaten, never "through".'

Steve gave me his recipe for 'mock' salmon one afternoon while we were finishing my bag lanyard. I remembered one Sunday he brought a large dish into the mess-deck, and gave me an advance spoonful to taste, asking me what I thought it was. The dish contained a mound of something pink in colour, and I had no hesitation in replying that of course it was salmon. The cook laughed and said we had no salmon aboard. His 'salmon' was made from corned beef, a little vinegar and tinned tomato juice. His recipe for this dish was two parts corned beef to one of tomato juice, with a dash of vinegar, salt and pepper to taste. Few people, I am sure, could have told the difference between this 'mock' salmon, and the real thing.

Another time I was leaning against the galley door at cocoa time, with a pot of cocoa in my hand. The cook and I were watching the antics of a venturesome gull, who boldly flew down and stole a piece of cod's liver from the deck, where it had fallen from the liver basket.

'We never attempt to harm the gulls,' Steve remarked, following my eyes as we watched the gull fly aloft with its prize, only to be mobbed by about a dozen of its fellows. 'You see, in the winter,' he continued, 'they are the only friends we have out here, and they keep us company. In the old days, trawlermen and smacks-men believed that, when they died, their souls returned again in the shape of a gull. So we never begrudge them a fish or two, or even a piece of liver.' Fishermen, even today, are very superstitious.

During the long steam home from the White Sea grounds, the *Stella Arcturus* had a little trouble in the engine-room, and we put into Tromso, Norway, for spares. The Skipper had radioed ashore and we hoped the parts would be waiting for us, as we did not expect to remain alongside for long.

I went ashore with Steve, the cook, and two others, to visit the ship chandler's store further in the town. The streets of Tromso were deserted, which was only to be expected as it was not then 5 a.m. A thin drizzle of rain was falling, which quickly soaked us all. I was surprised to find the store open at this time of the morning, but the chandler told us he had been open since 2 a.m. getting supplies ready for the mail-boat in the harbour.

We had been in the shop about half an hour when we heard two long blasts from the *Arcturus*'s siren, which was a pre-arranged signal she was ready to sail. As the chandler was going down to the harbour with supplies, the cook and I, along with the others, piled into the back of his truck, and rode down to the water's edge. We were only too glad of the lift, as the rain was pouring down by then. No sooner had the cook unloaded his box of supplies and scrambled over the rail than the warps were cast off, and we steamed slowly out of the harbour, passing anchored seaplanes in the fiord.

Little more remains to be told of the voyage. My kitbag handle was finished and fixed to my bag. We were all waiting with our gear at our feet, as the *Stella Arcturus* slowly nosed her way through the lock-pit of the St. Andrew's Dock, Hull. Steve Roberts appeared, looking clean and pink, and freshly shaved, with his 'kipper' tie – complete with bathing beauty, blowing around his left ear. We talked for a few minute longer, then he gave me a firm handshake, said 'Goodbye', threw his dunnage ashore, and jumped after it almost as soon as the warps were fast to the dockside. With one last wave of his hand, and tie still blowing in the wind, he vanished round the corner of a dockside building, and out of my life for ever. That was the last time I saw Steve. I heard of him from time to time, but that was his last trip on the *Stella Arcturus*. He had decided to make the break from his father-in-law's ship, and changed ships twice in one year.

Finally, he joined the trawler *Lorella* as cook in the autumn of 1954. That winter of 1954-55 was particularly severe for icing conditions on the fishing grounds. In January, 1955, I was shocked to hear that two Hull trawlers, the *Roderigo* and the *Lorella,* had both been lost with all hands off the north coast of Iceland. Steve Roberts lies now in the wrecked trawler *Lorella*. At the bottom of the Arctic ocean, but a worn lanyard on an old kit-bag reminds me of him still . . .

Stella Arcturus:
Built in 1946 by Cochrane & Sons Ltd. of Selby.
Yard No. 1309.
Owners: St. Andrew's Steam Fishing Co., Ltd.
Launched as *St. Bartholomew*, 21 February, 1946.
Fishing No: H216. Official No: 180475
177.6 ft. long x 30.2 ft. breadth.
216 net tons, 579 gross tons.
Sold to Charleson-Smith Ltd., and renamed *Stella Arcturus,* 14 September, 1946
Sold to Boyd Line Ltd., 13 April, 1967, and 3 May, 1967, renamed *Arctic Outlaw*.
Laid up at Hull 5 September, 1968, and sold for scrap to P. W. McLellan of Glasgow.

LAST VOYAGE – *LOCH DOON*

A two-inch column of print was the simple epitaph of a once well-known Hull trawler. The report said: 'Two of the oldest steam trawlers in the fleet of Hellyer Bros. Ltd. are to be dry docked before beginning their last voyage. They are to be towed to Dunston on Tyne for breaking up . . .The two ships due to make their final trip are the *Loch Doon* and the *Brutus*. They have been laid up in St. Andrew's Dock, Hull, for almost two years, because they were considered to be no longer economically serviceable.'

On 18 January, 1952, the *Loch Doon*, built at Aberdeen in 1949, and then not quite three-years-old, sailed from St. Andrew's Dock, Hull, bound for the Greenland fishing grounds. She looked extremely smart with her dark green hull and grained 'wood effect' bridge and upper works, as she steamed out of the lock-pit on her much publicised voyage.

Under the command of Skipper Syd Sparkes, she was to prove to the industry that commercial fishing in Greenland waters was reasonably safe and feasible during the winter months. Leaving Spurn behind she sailed north and then west around Scotland. Round the tip of Greenland, past Cape Farewell, she went, then up the Davis Strait almost to Baffin Bay, braving dense pack-ice, and ice-bergs which they reported on their return were '. . . as big as the Albert Hall'. The *Loch Doon* had steamed further north in her search for fish than any British trawler had ever done at that season of the year. Usually, Greenland fishing was only attempted from about July to late October, and this pioneering voyage was in the nature of an experiment.

On 11 February, 1952, the *Loch Doon*, her green hull scarred by the Greenland ice-floes, sailed home to Hull and into the headlines of scores of

The Hull trawler Loch Doon *(1949).*

(Memory Lane, Hull)

Loch Doon *showing Hellyer Bros. logo on the funnel.*

(David Buckley Collection, Fleetwood)

newspapers. Far more important than her own individual success were the implications of the trip: she had pioneered the way for other trawlers of the future.

The *Loch Doon* and her crew had proved beyond doubt that the passage to the rich Greenland fishing grounds was not, as was previously believed, impossible during the winter months. Hardships, fog, ice and other hazards would have to be overcome, but the *Loch Doon* opened the way for other trawlers to follow. One national newspaper said of the *Loch Doon* and her crew: 'This is the spirit which sent Drake out in his cockleshell to sail uncharted seas. This is the spirit we need today.'

Within three years of this pioneering voyage, the first large factory freezer, the *Fairtry,* returned on 4 July, 1954, from her maiden voyage after fishing the same rich fishing grounds, In the years since then, more and larger freezer trawlers fish the same waters. All following where the little *Loch Doon* went, the first winter venturer of them all.

The *Loch Doon*'s days of glory are long since gone, her early pioneering voyage is hardly remembered today. The oldest members of that crew are now retired, and even the youngest of her crew on that Greenland voyage of 1952 will now be in their 50s. What of *Loch Doon*? She retired herself in 1970 and was laid up at the west end of St. Andrew's Dock for many months, until taken by tug to be dry docked in King George Dock for a brief survey prior to the tow to the breaker's yard.

It was while she was tied up in King George Dock, Hull, that I went aboard her for a brief look round. It was a grey, rainy day in late April, 1972, a day as grey as the colour of her hull; this was because she wore the grey colour scheme of Hellyer Bros. for the last few years of her useful life.

She looked neglected, tired and careworn, a real old lady. Her once clean decks were slimy and greasy with thick engine-oil. There was rust everywhere, and great flakes of paint were peeling from the upper bridge and engine-room casing. The ladder leading up to the bridge was dangerously loose. A large block hung down from the bridge top, swaying slowly in the wind, like the pendulum of a large clock that has almost run down. The bridge was a gutted ruin, with broken windows, green brass-work, smashed engine-room telegraph glass, trampled papers, and litter everywhere. A red and yellow signal flag hung out of the pigeonholes of the flag locker. The flag was the only clean item on board. In the radio room a tattered chart lay crumpled underfoot. A grimy note-pad still bore a scribbled message from the last fishing voyage, and a book on radio call-signs lay open and damp beneath a broken port glass.

Even the Skipper's berth was no different. The mahogany woodwork and fittings, once well-kept and polished, were now a shambles of scratched and half-opened drawers, full of scattered newspapers and damp magazines. A broken fire-extinguisher lay on the rusting wire springs of the Skipper's empty bunk. On the chart table, amidst a wad of damp paper and other litter, stood a pint bottle of cough mixture, still half-full, its label torn and peeling, a lone survivor among the wreckage.

On the bridge again, I gave a last glance around at the dirty matting on the deck, the loose ends of dozens of electric wires hanging from the bulkheads, and the broken light bulbs in battered fittings. A gust of wind blew through a gaping bridge window, bringing with it a spray of rain, as I turned to leave. The trawlermen who steered the *Loch Doon* from the bridge for more than 20 years had gone their separate ways. The wheel was lashed down with new cordage, ready for the tug to tow the vessel to her final anchorage.

The April rain dripped from the bridge, making ripples in the rainbow colours of the oily water which lay in pools on her decks. So I left the *Loch Doon* to her memories; she'd had her moment of glory, she'd had her epitaph. There was nothing more to see. Her days were over, her last voyage was about to begin.

Loch Doon:
Built in 1949 by Alex. Hall & Co., Ltd., Aberdeen.
Yard No: 729.
Owners: Caledonian Fishing Co., Ltd. (Managers Hellyer Bros.).
Fishing No: H101. Official No: 183422.
180.1 ft. long x 30.2 ft. breadth
245 tons net, 670 tons gross.
Transferred to Loch Fishing Co. Ltd., 19 October, 1959.
Transferred to Hellyer Bros., 29 June, 1966.
Withdrawn from Registry and laid up, 24 November, 1971 .
May, 1972, towed to yard of Clayton & Davie, Dunston-on-Tyne for scrap.

Glossary of Nautical Terms

A.B.	Able Bodied seaman.
Aft	Towards the stern of the vessel.
Amidships	Midway between the bow and the stern. Midships is the order to put the rudder fore and aft.
Astern	Behind the vessel.
Athwart	From side to side.
Awash	A vessel, wreck, rock or shoal that waves constantly wash over.
Ballast	Iron, lead or stone placed in the bottom of a ship to increase stability.
Beacon	Navigation light on shore or rocks.
Beam-ends	When a vessel is forced by wind or sea on to her side.
Bearing	Direction of object or ship at sea expressed in compass direction.
Bowsprit	Large timber spar foxed over the bow for triangular head sails.
Broach-to	To come into the wind and get broadside into a trough of the sea,
Buoy	Floating beacon with name, shape, colour, light or bell.
Cable	Nautical measurement of 100 fathoms (200 yards). Sometimes a chain or rope attached to an anchor.
Chart	Map of coastline showing marks and sea depths.
Davits	Steel cranes for lowering or hoisting lifeboats.
Dead-Reckoning	Position found by calculating course and speed of the vessel. Not very reliable.
Dolphin	A piled structure of timber or steel in the middle of a dock, used for mooring or turning a vessel.
Dunnage	A seaman's clothes and belongings. Also loose timber spread on the bottom of a ship's hold to keep the cargo off the damp bottom of the hold.
Fathom	Nautical measurement of six feet.
Fishroom	Hold of a trawler where the catch is stowed. Usually refrigerated.
Fore and Aft	In line with the keel. Lengthways of the ship.
Galley	A ship's kitchen where the food is prepared.
Knot	One nautical mile per hour.
Lead-line	A cylindrical lead weight with a concave, hollow base filled with tallow or grease. When it is lowered on a long line, a sample of sand or shingle from the sea-bed sticks to the tallow and shows the type of bottom. The line has markers at intervals showing the depth.
Lifebuoy	Circular ring of cork. A life preserver.
Line	A small rope, always called a line at sea. Log-line; Heaving line.
Log	A brass instrument rather like a clock face which records the speed of the vessel. Attached to the recorder is a long line at the end of which is a small cylinder with curved fins that revolves.
Pooped	When a high sea comes on board over the stern of a vessel.
Run	A day's run or total distance covered in 24 hours.
Started	When riveted steel plates or decking buckle under pressure.